CREATIVE
HOMEOWNER®

design ideas for
DECORATIVE
Concrete & Stone

CREATIVE HOMEOWNER®, Upper Saddle River, New Jersey

DESIGN IDEAS FOR DECORATIVE CONCRETE & STONE
AUTHORS: Ellen Frankel & Mervyn Kaufman
SENIOR EDITOR: Kathie Robitz
SENIOR DESIGNER: Glee Barre
DESIGNER: Stephanie Phelan
ASSISTANT EDITOR: Evan Lambert
EDITORIAL ASSISTANTS: Jen Calvert (proofreading)
    Robyn Poplasky (photo research)
INDEXER: Schroeder Indexing Services
FRONT COVER PHOTOGRAPHY: (top) coutesy of Art & Maison, photo: Sergio Fama; (bottom left) courtesy of Sonoma Cast Stone; (bottom center) design and photo: Brukoff Design Associates; (bottom right) Anne Gummerson
INSIDE FRONT COVER PHOTOGRAPHY: (*top*) Anne Gummerson; (*bottom*) Cheng Design
BACK COVER PHOTOGRAPHY: (*top*) Paul Bardagjy; (*bottom right*) Paul Bardagjy; (*bottom left*) photo and design: Brukoff Design Associates
INSIDE BACK COVER PHOTOGRAPHY: Mark Samu

CREATIVE HOMEOWNER
PRESIDENT: Brian Toolan
VP/EDITORIAL DIRECTOR: Timothy O. Bakke
PRODUCTION MANAGER: Kimberly H. Vivas
ART DIRECTOR: David Geer
MANAGING EDITOR: Fran J. Donegan

Printed in China

Current Printing (last digit)
10 9 8 7 6 5 4 3 2 1
Design Ideas for Decorative Concrete & Stone, First Edition
Library of Congress Control Number: 2006924716
ISBN-10: 1-58011-312-5
ISBN-13: 978-1-58011-312-0

CREATIVE HOMEOWNER®
A Division of Federal Marketing Corp.
24 Park Way
Upper Saddle River, NJ 07458
www.creativehomeowner.com

Dedication

For our respective families, generous in providing support

and encouragement, and particularly for Tucker

Acknowledgments

We are indebted to Stephanie Phelan, who brought her

intellgence and sophisticated design sense to every page; to a

stellar list of photographers, manufacturers, designers, and

architects, who shone the spotlight on their best work and

shared such beautiful images with us; and certainly to our editor,

Kathie Robitz, for her guidance and trust.

Contents

ABOVE Limestone—as pavers and as hand-shaped blocks on exterior walls—leads to this house's gracious front door.

RIGHT Marble was used to create a bathroom's custom counter, which encircles a sink set into a cherry base.

BELOW Molded pilasters and bulls-eye ornamentation add formal touches to a marble fireplace set on a slate hearth.

The choices are mind-blowing and often so extensive you don't know what to do. You visit a showroom or a home center and look at walls of samples—and scratch your head. There is marble and granite and lots of other beautiful stones. There is also concrete, now available in appealing colors. What's right for your needs? What's worth your money? You look around for help and finally realize the onus is on you. You have to make the final selection. That's where *Design Ideas for Decorative Concrete & Stone* comes in. Let this book guide you, for in chapter after chapter you'll see how concrete and

Introduction

various types of stone, including man-made versions, look in a series of beautiful settings. And you'll learn how well each product functions—under foot or when used as trim or a work surface. Which materials require regular maintenance? Which need special care? Which can be mostly left alone? By the time you've turned the last page, you'll know as much as you need to about all of these marvelous materials, many of which were formed under ground millions of years ago. You'll be fully prepared to make the best choices for all those improvements that are so long overdue.

Commercially, it not only frames buildings, but as precast modular blocks it often adorns building facades. Until recently, homeowners knew concrete as poured foundations, driveways, and basement floors. But advanced technology has made this viable and once barely visible product part of a variety of decorative home situations. Why? Because it's not only easy to mold and shape but, if skillfully worked, can imitate any natural product. And once thought of as dull to look at, being mainly gray, and rough to touch, it is now produced in a range of colors and finishes. Where's the concrete? Today, it's everywhere.

Where's the Concrete?

▮ shapely stunners ▮ cool, sleek, utterly modern ▮ color it concrete ▮ ▮ outdoor possibilties ▮ ▮ for decoration ▮

Elegantly shaped, this fireplace surround tapers gradually toward the floor. The opening frames a view from the living room through a similar-size fireplace opening in the adjoining dining room.

Whether it surrounds a sunken tub or frames a fireplace, concrete has a chameleon-like capability. It can assume many forms and be colored integrally, painted, stained, or accented to match or blend with other decorating elements. Moreover, it can be adapted to take on any mood or style, from sleek and shiny to rough and rustic, from convincingly traditional to unmistakably contemporary.

Because concrete really is molded, it can be made to assume shapes that would be impossible to achieve with almost any other material. Moreover, it has the potential for being not only water-resistant but truly stain-resistant as well.

shapely stunners

TOP LEFT A one-piece tub and deck, set into a windowed niche, makes a sleek statement, its surface reflecting light from the morning sun.

LEFT Counter and sink in a luscious tone are cast in a single piece. The concrete's lustrous sheen results from repeated diamond-pad polishings.

BELOW AND OPPOSITE These fireplaces make totally different decorating statements. One has a raised hearth and a deep mantel for displaying collectibles; the other has angled side panels and a fireproof concrete firebox.

I I I I I I I I I I I I I I I I I I I I I I I I southwestern style I I I I I I I I I I I I I I I

worked **l**ike **c**lay

Because it shapes easily by hand, concrete has become a favorite of many sculptors. It's a medium that can be manipulated when wet, turning mundane objects like the sink at left into personalized works of handcrafted and colorful art.

ABOVE A rough-surfaced concrete fireplace is the focal point of the master bedroom in a log-built home. The fireplace front rises through the ceiling, becoming an exterior chimney that extends above the roof. Abstract flames have been painted around the fireplace opening.

OPPOSITE Concrete walls, floor, and staircase give the foyer of this desert-country home a warm, earthy look. With some ceramic tile trim as accents, the concrete stairs have hand-painted risers that look deceptively like individually hand-set tiles.

versatility **p**lus

Molded concrete is widely used in creating mantels, hearths, and fireplace surrounds. It can be used to line fireboxes as well, but only if a concrete specifically formulated for fiery heat is specified—or if the fireboxes are heat-insulated or lined with hardy firebrick. Everyday concrete is likely to crack and disintegrate if exposed to ultra-high temperatures over time. In a fire, concrete may lose some of its integrity, but as it cannot be ignited easily, it is considered a fire-safe product. Also, it presents a virtually impenetrable barrier to water, which is why it is now being used so often in crafting sinks. Square, spherical, sloping, straight, scooped, or flat—there is no sink shape that is beyond concrete's capacity.

Concrete is amazingly versatile in appearance. You can achieve a look that's smooth and seamless or opt for concrete tiles for a different effect. In its raw state, concrete is porous and vulnerable. With a proper sealer and careful application, so every surface is coated, concrete becomes capable of resisting water and stains.

BELOW A modern take on a traditional farm sink, this version sits neatly between two sections of countertop. Concrete has the advantage of being able to mimic, in tone and shape, almost any other like material. This particular style can be ordered with a perforated pad, in stainless steel, that's embedded to reinforce the bottom against heavy use.

RIGHT In a symmetrically designed space, a raised fireplace in white concrete meshes beautifully with the white and dark-stained woods surrounding it. The designer created a two-level mantel for the owner to display candles and collectibles.

| | | | | crisp and contemporary | | | | | | | | | | | | | | | | | |

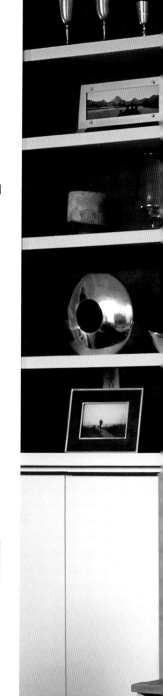

ABOVE A custom-designed polished-concrete wall notches into this contemporary-style living room. A floor-to-ceiling design, its solidity and square-cornered design are reflected in the shape of the large coffee table. First, it has a floor-level fireplace opening with a shallow mantel above it. Second, it has a recessed upper portion with a cutout made to fit a TV.

RIGHT Three elements make up this design: a sleek concrete counter, a deep sink, and a stainless-steel drain-board integrated into the countertop. Concrete is so flexible, insists the fabricator, that architects and designers can do anything they imagine.

LEFT Double sinks in a spacious bath are wide rectangles scooped out of a single extended countertop. A modest backsplash and a complementary section of counter extend beyond the sink area to partly conceal the toilet and create wall-to-wall unity.

BELOW Concrete in a rich earth tone sweeps across the countertop and snack bar surfaces and wraps around a set-in cooktop. The main sink, which angles sharply off the primary food-prep counter, is lined with stainless steel for sturdiness and durability.

|||||||| contrasting shapes, tones, and textures ||||||||

ABOVE Countertops in this eat-in kitchen were poured and shaped in place. For texture and sheen, all of these surfaces were sprinkled with marble dust before the concrete hardened and was sealed.

LEFT Dark wood that frames the window and tub deck presents a textured look in contrast to the smooth primary materials. A notched concrete deck surrounds the tub.

OPPOSITE An example of elegantly mixed materials, a wall-hung concrete counter supports a stainless-steel vessel-style sink. The sink's shape is reflected in the large wood-framed mirror hanging above it.

LEFT Three shades of acid stain were used on this columned lanai's elegant floor. A stamping process was applied to create the look of polished marble.

ABOVE An acid stain gives a rich tone to the concrete floor in this U-shape kitchen. The poured floor was stained to resemble a diamond arrangement of tiles in two tones.

ABOVE RIGHT Hand-set, huge slabs of concrete veined to look like marble were individually cast and put in place to create a uniform floor design with pencil-thin grouting.

RIGHT Random-shaped concrete, tinted in three different tones, was polished to create the gleaming floor in a California home. The floor sweeps dramatically toward the kitchen.

possibilities **u**nder **f**oot

There was a time when a concrete floor was something you covered with another flooring material, such as wall-to wall carpeting. Concrete was only left bare in the basement where it may or may not have been painted. That was then, of course. Now the possibilities are limitless. With new acid stains, stamps, and special-formula water-based paints, an ugly-duckling concrete floor can be easily turned into a decorating swan. Cut into tiles, thin layers of concrete can be applied, like pieces in a jigsaw puzzle, to create intricate and geometric patterns. Curves and swirls, too, are possible, because of the more sophisticated than ever cutting, polishing, and honing machinery, which is the key to concrete's vaunted versatility.

||||||||||||||||| a sink for every special need ||||||||||||

LEFT A notched-out concrete countertop and backsplash make
a sleek statement in this bath with
mirror-mounted fittings. A white
ceramic vessel-style sink and a
glass shower stall add lightness to
the mix of tones and materials.

TOP LEFT Set against an outdoor
background of stones and rocks,
this individually shaped lavatory
sink has the look of antiquity—
"imperfect as the hands that made
it," says the fabricator. Colored pigments added to the concrete mix
produced a tone that runs all the
way through this product.

TOP RIGHT Despite their contrasting colors, there is a
seamless look to this pairing of rectangular sink and
countertop, both molded concrete. A mosaic-tile backsplash adds color and pattern, a compelling mix.

ABOVE Despite its splashy setting, this one-piece concrete sink and countertop is a down-to-earth solution
to bathroom needs. This striking console has a sculptural look, with its deeply scooped-out sink supported
by wrought-iron legs and crossbars.

LEFT Gleaming white, in actuality and in its reflection,
a large concrete vanity sink with a curved bottom has a
rim wide enough to hold most essential bath needs.

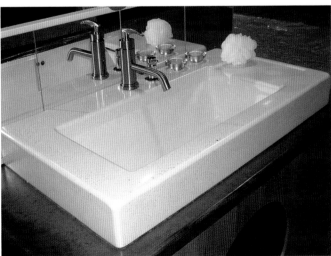

Because it can assume such extraordinary shapes and present such attractive surfaces, concrete has become a favorite of architects and designers who prefer the purity of contemporary style. Straight lines, angles, curves—all are possible with a product so malleable. The most striking of these brilliantly cast products looks as if it was just produced from freshly carved stone. Concrete can also be turned into claylike objects by professionals skilled at working with the medium. Using basic tools it can also be carved.

One-piece sinks and countertops are easily attainable and can be created without the telltale seams that often distinguish other materials. Countertops are today's most popular use of concrete in the home—mainly because they can be cast in place and because each can be made special. An integral drainboard can be carved into countertop areas beside the sink; similarly, narrow metal bars can be implanted near a range or cooktop for use as a trivet when hot pots are removed from the burners, oven, or broiler; and decorative particles—colorful pebbles, odd-shaped stones, bits of glass, marble chips, chunks of tile, even leaves—can be embedded in concrete as richly effective decorative accents.

cool, sleek, utterly modern

ABOVE A concrete pier with a textured surface supports the end of a countertop that sweeps around the periphery of a sleekly designed contemporary kitchen. Steel stools repeat the gray tone. The curves and angles show off the versatility of this highly malleable material.

RIGHT In another virtuoso display of versatility, a wall-mounted concrete sink with a large concave bowl attests to the delicate shaping that produced it. This is an example of the kind of custom work that makes concrete such an attractive material for consumers and so popular with designers.

OPPOSITE In a bathroom tour de force, a concrete-topped vanity, with two curved-bottom integral sinks and a center grooming space, intersects with a concrete tub deck. The floor presents an arrangement of giant cast-concrete tiles with matching grout.

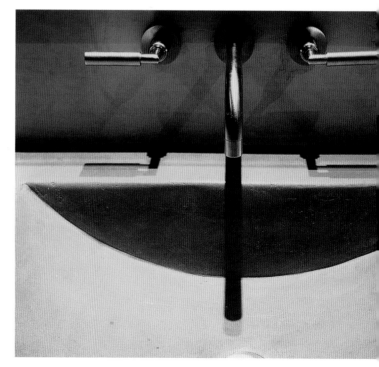

LEFT AND BOTTOM CENTER A huge expanse of concrete countertop is functionally interrupted by a slightly lowered drainboard that flows out of the sink.

OPPOSITE BOTTOM LEFT A slab-supported concrete dining table has a roughened surface.

BELOW Installed beside a traditional freestanding tub, a squared-off contemporary-style concrete vanity has hollowed-out spaces for bathroom storage. Counter and vanity are one; the undermount sink is in a complementary material.

RIGHT: A glass wall separates a breakfast bar from a butler's pantry, with its own stainless-steel undermount sink. Both concrete countertops are curved and custom made to fit very tight spaces. The two curved counters, mounted at different levels, would form a circle if actually pulled together.

at last it can be told

▌ **Concrete's big secret** is that there is no secret. A skilled craftsman is needed if concrete is to be used to achieve a particularly special design, but the material itself can be produced successfully in any workshop or garage. Note that concrete and cement are not synonymous terms, although people often refer to one when they mean the other. Cement is a powderlike material that acts as a bonding agent. Concrete is what is obtained when mixing cement, sand, and aggregate (crushed stone or gravel) with water. The result dries quickly without being fired, and even though it contains water it can, with appropriate additives, be made water-resistant.

▌ **Color choices continue to grow.** In addition, endlessly individual edge treatments are possible with concrete, and many a concrete contractor has built a reputation on being able to produce unique treatments for demanding clients. Similarly, concrete specialists are able to create veined looks.

ABOVE In a home office, a concrete counter extends beyond the cabinet and into an adjacent wall.

LEFT A long, shallow concrete sink serves two people in this master bath. The sink bottom slopes so that water runs into the drain.

RIGHT Molded in one piece, this deep, slightly tapered soaking tub makes a stand-alone statement.

OPPOSITE Seemingly an extension of the concrete walls beyond it, a peninsula stands at the entrance to an open-design kitchen.

OPPOSITE AND BELOW Tapered concrete piers support the beamed roof that rises dramatically above this glass-wrapped house. Inside, concrete on walls and floor are a foil for the random-shaped glass windows and pine beams.

ABOVE A white porcelain tub is undermounted in a raised concrete tub deck backed by a concrete wall with a niche that holds shampoos and bath salts.

RIGHT A wide, rectangular molded bathroom sink with two bottom surfaces (one sloping toward the center), meet to form a full width drain, making a strong case for the flexibility of concrete.

I I I I I I molded marvels I I I I I I I I I I I I I I I I I I I I I I I I I I I I I I I I I I I I I I I I I I I I I I I I I I I I I I I I

ABOVE Solving the problem of
what to do with a large-screen TV,
here it's placed in a niche above a
similarly shaped concrete fireplace.

RIGHT Two box-like sinks, each
with deeply scooped bowls and wall-
mounted fittings, are set against a
concrete wall. Their graphic veining
adds a decorative punch to a mostly
white bath. The sinks rest on a black
concrete counter hung on the wall.

FAR LEFT Two faucets—one a standard gooseneck, the other designed as a pot filler—are mounted in this elongated counter. A grooved drainboard molded into one section of concrete allows water spills to flow back into the undermount sink.

LEFT Brilliantly molded like a tapering tower, a freestanding vanity sink set into its own base is the result of a single concrete mold. Hand polishing achieved the lustrous surface on the circular bowl.

BELOW Concrete counters wrap around a U-shape kitchen, then drop down to form a long dining table, supported by a stainless-steel-wrapped column. Separating dining and cooking areas, the dining tabletop was made slightly thicker than the kitchen counters.

IIIIIIIIIIIII shapes and extensions IIIIIIIIIIIIIIIIIIIIIIIIII

The best and most reliable way to apply color to concrete is through a process known as acid staining, although no acid is actually used. To create permanent concrete colors, chemical stains are what are actually applied. These are mainly metallic salts in an acidic, water-based solution that react with free lime deposits that are buried in the concrete compound.

In the coloring process, the acid contained in the stain penetrates the upper surface of the concrete mixture, allowing the salts to reach the lime deposits (which are technically calcium hydroxide). The color change is the result of a slow and gradual chemical reaction. Concrete with a cement content that is high in lime tends to yield richer color.

color **it concrete**

ABOVE Colors collide beautifully in a designer kitchen, with veined concrete counters set into end sections molded of yellow concrete. A mosaic backsplash adds visual excitement.

RIGHT In the same kitchen as above, the stainless-steel gas cooktop contrasts with the matte-finish concrete countertop's veining, which resembles polished marble.

OPPOSITE As a departure from conventional kitchen planning, the designer angled the island, widened it at the end, and defined the dining zone by juxtaposing concrete in a contrasting color. Concrete squares in varying tones comprise the floor.

∎∎ choose a tone to match your mood and style ∎∎∎∎∎∎∎∎∎∎∎

ABOVE Acid-stained a brilliant aquamarine, this concrete-topped island has a two-sided cabinet with multiple rows of storage drawers—shallow for tableware, deep for pots and pans. The countertop extension, supported by a pair of stainless-steel legs, is ideal for quick meals. Or, during dinner party preparation, it can serve as an additional work zone.

RIGHT The main sink in the same kitchen as above has tapering grooves cut into the concrete to allow spilled liquids to flow into the undermount basin. Concrete can be waterproof and heat resistant. If concrete is sealed properly, food spills can be wiped away effectively without leaving stains.

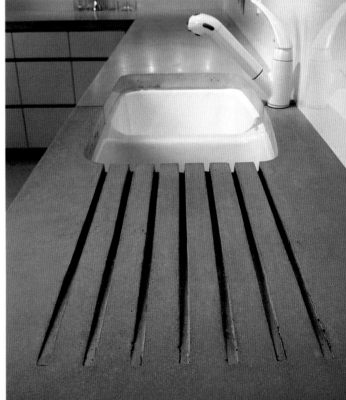

ABOVE An ample sink is undermounted into this bright aqua concrete vanity, which is framed in dazzling mosaic tile. The cabinet itself hangs on the wall, leaving standing room below. Flooring is scored concrete in a tone to match the counter.

LEFT An aggregate mix of particles and concrete brings texture and color accents to a vanity cut out to make room for a rectangular undermount sink. To bring the aggregate to the surface, a countertop like this must be ground and polished.

routine care and cleaning

- **DO** use cutting boards when chopping and slicing as you prepare foods to cook. You can't mar the concrete surface, but you can damage the sealer, the element that's applied to resist water and stains.
- **DON'T** place hot pans on concrete surfaces. The heat won't affect the material, but it can damage or discolor the sealer.
- **DO** apply wax once a week during the first month you own your concrete counter or sink, then twice a year thereafter. Buff regularly with a soft cloth to enhance the shine on the surface and increase sealer durability.
- **DON'T** use abrasive soaps, pads or cleansers to clean up spills. Mixed with warm water, mild soaps and non-ammoniated detergents work best.
- **DO** use concrete products with confidence. They can easily be repaired, colored, sealed, and finished again.

bright idea
discovery!

Developing Portland cement, circa 1900, led to the creation of concrete, which revolutionized the building industry.

LEFT Dazzling color marks this designer kitchen. Here, the concrete countertop in a rich earth tone abuts a backsplash of mosaic tile that wraps around much of the kitchen.

BOTTOM The designer stained the cabinet doors and drawer fronts to complement the concrete counter, which angles seamlessly around the periphery of this grand-scale kitchen.

RIGHT The professional-style range is a drop-in model framed by a one-piece concrete countertop, with a strip of concrete behind the appliance to link the sections. Selected wood cabinet doors and drawer fronts are stained in whimsical patterns with recurring motifs.

notable caveats

Although concrete's possible applications are seemingly limitless, there is wisdom in using the material only where it works best.

▌ **Smooth finishes,** ideal for sinks, countertops, and tabletops, should be avoided on floors or paved areas that can become slippery when wet.

▌ **Rough-textured and surface-colored finishes** are best for fireplace surrounds, wall panels, or backsplashes—surfaces that are unlikely to become clogged with dirt or show wear with hard, repeated use over time.

▌ **Concrete sinks** may be less practical than other products in a sink that gets heavy use or must be scrubbed often. Bathroom placement may be smarter.

LEFT Two tones of acid-stained concrete comprise the floor of this dining-living space. The dining area is defined by the more intense tone, which acts like an area rug.

BELOW This bath for two has luster and sparkle juxtaposed with the squares of concrete on the floor and concrete counters under the vessel sinks. The curved wall is faced in mosaic tile that adds color. Mosaics at the baseboard rim the concrete floor and wrap the room in borders, even below the crown molding.

RIGHT A movable grate extends partly across the gracefully separated concrete double sinks.

OPPOSITE BOTTOM The manufacturer of this one-piece powder room counter and sink created the freeform basin in a suggested fish design. Concrete containing purple pigment was poured and vibrated to remove any bubbles, then allowed to dry.

custom curves

sink shape

- **Sculpting large sinks** or any complex shapes requires skill and judgment. There is a limit to how much concrete can be stretched and bent without cracking, confirming that professional experience is needed before tackling large-scale projects involving concrete.
- **Cast concrete is produced** industrially on a large scale, but it's possible for anyone with good potting skills to craft special-shaped sinks or any small-scale concrete objects.
- **You can also create** a special or unusual shape by making your own flexible mold. Apply liquid latex or urethane rubber onto the shape you've chosen; pour, spray, or brush on the liquid; let it harden; then mold concrete to the surface.

bright idea

carve it

Using the tip of a nail or the edge of a knife or spoon, you can create distinctive concrete shapes. Remember to work with concrete that is stiff but not yet hard. For added sheen, sprinkle with marble dust.

color cues

I **Add liquid** or powdered pigment while the concrete is being mixed. But remember: liquid pigment is more likely to yield solid, even color, all the way through the concrete.

I **Achieve bright** and vivid colors by starting with white cement.

I **Acid stains** on concrete are long lasting and fade-resistant, although their color power is only surface-deep.

I **Water-based paints** are brushed or sprayed on soon after concrete hardens, but it should dry for a month before any oil-based paint is applied.

ABOVE A pair of V-shaped vessel sinks are set into a solid-concrete console in a master bath. The highly polished sinks are smooth to the touch, in contrast to the console, which has a roughened surface. The same rich tone extends throughout.
I
BELOW AND OPPOSITE Geometric shapes dominate this extraordinary bathroom, the work of a West Coast designer. The vanity (below) has drawers that mimic the cabinet's tapered shape; the sinks angle even farther outward. Another concrete creation (opposite) has a niche for shampoos. Beside the shower, a tub is set into a concrete deck. The floor is a series of large concrete squares in various colors.

dramatic design set in concrete

super surfaces

- **Add shells,** bits of stone, scrap metal, or glass shards to a concrete mix to achieve a variegated look, as pictured.
- **Inlays,** which can be any object or motif, will put a special stamp on a concrete installation.
- **Grinding** a dry, hardened concrete surface will make elements you've added more apparent and, at the same time, create a flat, smooth surface.
- **Polishing,** which can produce either a glossy or satin finish, is done with diamond pads on a machine polisher or by carefully using wet-dry sandpaper.

LEFT This living room was given a single splash of color: a wall of purple concrete blocks that includes a fireplace opening and a free-floating mantel. The wall design includes storage space for logs, concealed by a retractable door.

TOP Shaped counters throughout this kitchen demonstrate concrete's ability to be straight or angular. The counters' warm earth tone is sparked by ceramic tiles that beautifully express the wisdom of mixing materials.

ABOVE One sink, two faucets—this is a his-and-hers arrangement that provides room for two in a single compact space. Creating a single long, sloping sink is a dramatic flourish that also shows off the beauty of concrete molded in a very special way.

RIGHT A concrete counter angles around the corner of this kitchen, embracing a faucet and sink. The counter is accented by the designer's bold use of split colors on cabinet doors.

RIGHT Square but with a slight dip, this lav sink in a dark acid stain is mostly worked by hand to achieve its shape.

BOTTOM A yellow counter with a trough sink is the center-piece of this mirrored master bath. The sink's interior front surface angles down, creating a provocative concrete shape.

OPPOSITE Wood was used to add warmth and contrast here, softening the severity of the concrete curb, bench, and tub. The twin sinks have been scooped out of a concrete trough with a plateau of the same material separating them.

bright idea

cast beauty

This shallow molded sink was given unique coloration with a red oxide pigment that was applied integrally to the concrete mix.

the men who brought concrete home

Fu-Tung Cheng was not the first design professional to proclaim the decorative virtues of concrete. But his successes in bringing concrete into the homes of his clients in and around Berkeley, California, and in other parts of the country have made him one of concrete's principal proponents. Buddy Rhodes is another concrete pioneer in the Bay Area who helped launch the entry of concrete into the home. Still, Cheng's honest evaluation of the product has made him an authority who can be trusted. He believes:

▌ **No other material** offers as many opportunities for achieving creative looks for floors.

▌ **The best work** is done by professionals experienced in handling concrete in its many applications, shapes, and colors.

▌ **Colors that reflect** nature's palette work best; colors that are too bright have an artificial look and may become dated.

▌ **Trained specialists** are able to achieve unique special effects using various acrylic paints and dyes.

▌ **A wet mix** of concrete is more likely to shrink and crack after drying than a mix that is stiffer and less moist.

▌ **When adding** pebbles or stone fragments, wet them first for a firmer bond.

▌ **Inlays** will put a special stamp on any concrete installation. (Cheng likes to apply a small cut, polished fossil inlay to each of his concrete achievements.)

▌ **Commercial rubber stamps** can be used to make a concrete surface resemble brick or natural stone. But concrete looks best when it does not imitate other materials.

▌ **Grinding** a dry, hardened concrete surface will emphasize added detail and create an absolutely flat, smooth surface.

▌ **Polishing** concrete to a glossy or satin finish can be done by machine with diamond pads or by hand with wet-dry sandpaper. A polished floor requires less maintenance than a textured one.

Many of the same treatments that concrete contractors and design professionals attempt indoors are equally effective outdoors as well. The one big difference is that exterior surfaces are rarely as slick and shiny as those created indoors. Concrete pavers are often cast and set individually, just like natural stone. Or surfaces can be scored or carved to look

outdoor possibilities

like individual stones or bricks, set in place. And clever fabricators have learned to stamp on incised patterns and designs, further confirming concrete's enormous versatility.

OPPOSITE Concrete cast at the site, in this case the pool deck of an Arizona hideaway, was tinted a soft sand color. The stepping stones, though cast individually, received deep cuts while the concrete was hardening, as did the surrounding slabs.

BELOW The concrete deck outside a brick carriage house was crafted to look like rows of brick in multiple configurations. A power saw made cuts in the molded product, and each cut unit was roughened and scored.

I I I I I I I I I I I I I I I I concrete makes a marvelous mimic I I I I I

LEFT A mix of poured concrete and bricks forms these tranquil garden arches. The lily pond is bordered by large concrete pavers that alternate with grass patches the same size.

ABOVE Adding a golden glow to a partially glass-wrapped indoor-outdoor room with bright yellow upholstery, a yellow-dyed concrete console table set on two fat pedestals makes a stellar appearance.

RIGHT This concrete patio was heavily scored so that the slate-like pavers resemble singular blocks.

timeless textured looks

For a sophisticated look on paved outdoor surfaces, consider the different textures that can be created in concrete.

▎**A brushed surface** is achieved by dragging or pushing a special broom across poured concrete that has not yet hardened.
▎**A wash finish** can be done when new concrete has hardened just enough to bear weight. Water is applied to wash away a little of the upper layer.
▎**A stippled surface** is created by scattering rock salt or fertilizer pellets onto a slab that's still wet. When the concrete has hardened completely, the pellets will be washed away, and the finish will have a stippled look.

LEFT Concrete that's been warmly tinted was used to give the floor of this Southern home the look of polished terra-cotta. This is the covered porch, designed in a style with historical resonance in this region, with ceiling fans and adjustable windows.

BELOW Two tones of concrete were combined to produce this spacious outdoor area. Large slabs are intersected by narrow border strips, all of which have been given grout-like scoring. The surface was sealed, waxed, and buffed, becoming as elegant as any indoor installation.

RIGHT These walkways and patio areas are not the only concrete achievements here. The house itself, an architect-designed contemporary, features a poured-concrete facade.

oncrete has long been used in outdoor applications—planters, flower boxes, birdbaths,
and benches—in addition to the usual patios and
driveways. Now, it is indoors where the most
innovative concrete uses can be found. For even in
contemporary homes, some special ornamentation is usually required, not only for decoration
but for practical reasons as well. Shelves, benches,
pedestals, and fireplace mantels, plus a host of
handsome small objects are being made from
concrete by artisans challenged to use the product
in more and more new and inventive ways. What
motivates them? Concrete's unique warmth, initial malleability, and limitless color possibilities. In
these respects, the product is matchless.

for decoration

ABOVE LEFT This designed-for-one gracefully curved bench in
a custom-pressed finish is perfect for meditation.

ABOVE Here, striking mini-platforms add lively interest—in this
case, slim vases with bright flowers. Small boxes of concrete tiles
are cemented into place, then mounted at regular intervals.

LEFT Concrete-shaped planks, used as shelving for a collection
of pottery, add texture and make a statement of their own.

RIGHT This bench appears to be made of timber that has been
assembled, but it is actually a molded concrete piece of furniture. Additives ensure that outdoor pieces don't shrink as they
dry out over time, making them more water-tight.

object lessons

Concrete is no longer what it used to be—far from it. Now this once strictly utilitarian material is red-hot with designers who are using it as often inside the home as they are outside on the patio or driveway. Handsome small objects are being made, too, by artisans challenged to use it creatively because of its unique warmth, malleability and color possibilities. For example, look at the objects pictured below. Can these be concrete? A framed mirror, a long bench with a hollowed-out base, a circular table on an angular base—these are just a sampling of molded decorative objects today. Often they are being made to fool the eye.

▌ **Concrete is widely seen** in contemporary homes, where geometric shapes dominate and the texture provides contrast for the slickness. But as eclecticism continues to exercise its unending appeal, more and more concrete products are finding their way into homes where traditional style normally reigns.

▌ **Concrete really is chameleon-like.** It can be adapted to any shape or style, and by the way it is toned, textured and finished, it can be made to look like any other available material. No wonder architects, designers, and creative artists are attracted to it! Whether it's used indoors or out, concrete is king.

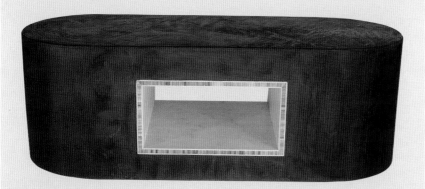

ABOVE Stone-faced lions form the ends of two giant concrete chairs, molded especially to give this sunny room a strong outdoor feel. The tabletop is also concrete, with a frame that matches the curvy wrought-iron base.

Since people first began harnessing nature to build walls, dwellings, and weapons, natural stone has been a material of choice—easily mined when quarries were discovered and easily cut and shaped with even the most basic tools. Indeed, stone is as old as planet Earth. The minerals that abound in natural stone evolve from the same minerals, liquids, and gases that pushed up to the earth's surface from within its core eons ago. Expert craftspeople now are able to manipulate stone for almost any use. Cutting and casting are only two methods of creating stone product.

Got to Get Stone

❚ rough and smooth ❚ walkways ❚
❚ kitchen cavalcade ❚ bath bonanza ❚
❚ hearth dreams ❚ refinements ❚

Cut and shaped by hand but left mostly rough to the touch, a pile of stones is transformed into a series of borders, as in the flower gardens on this seaside property.

Whatever its origins and whether it's hard or soft, stone possesses raw beauty enhanced by its ability to be manipulated. Natural stone occurs in the earth in a great many forms, but a few are more common than others. Sedimentary stone results from the actions of oceans, rivers, wind, and glaciers, creating enough pressure to allow rock beds to form. Metamorphic stone evolves from the impact of minerals, intense heat, and pressure to turn one type of stone into another. Igneous stone has volcanic origins. When boiling lava cools beneath the earth's surface, mineral gases and liquid minerals penetrate the stone, creating new crystalline forms.

rough and smooth

OPPOSITE Contrasting colors, shapes, and sizes mark the split-faced stones used to build this loggia, with its massive columns and geometrically patterned floor.

ABOVE A symmetrical arrangement of shaped stones shields the mechanism of an outdoor fountain whereon water is recirculated from the pond it flows into.

LEFT Stones in various textures and shapes were used to create this house facade. Smooth, flat stones form the arch above the window and radiate outward to create a patio surface. Rough fieldstones in random sizes have been cemented together to form the walls and window well.

LEFT Rough-cut stones flanking this delicate garden gate have a counterpart in the low wall along the entry walkway.

ABOVE A circle of sandstone in soft and variable tones creates a sunburst effect and accents a patio floor.

OPPOSITE LEFT Shielded from the sun, this small patio fireplace has emerald-toned squares of stone set into the stucco, edging the "mantel" and arched fireplace opening.

OPPOSITE FAR RIGHT Alfresco dining is always a treat, but on this green lava-stone tabletop, it becomes a special occasion. The patio floor is unpolished terra-cotta stone.

like clay in an artist's hand

Variations in texture and pattern were achieved here by unique arrangements of shaped and colored stone veneers. These tabletops present a sampling of possibilities—mosaic stones arranged in squares and diamonds, plus solid borders. Placed either indoors or outdoors, they should be coated with a penetrating sealer—to prevent stains and discoloration—and wiped regularly with a clean, soft cloth.

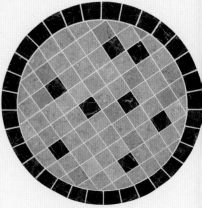

bright idea

good shape

Skilled artisans can work with stone to create compelling patterns and forms that are decorative as well as practical.

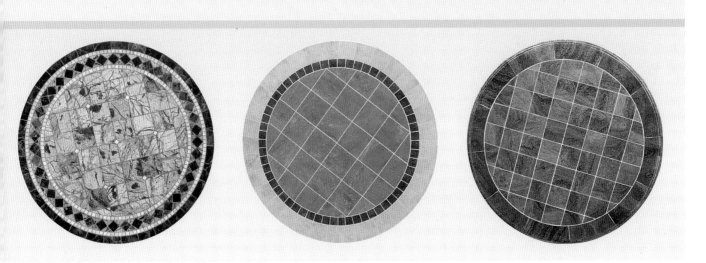

outdoor enhancements

OPPOSITE Like a sun-lit cave, this covered porch is shaped by large, split-faced stones, which not only frame open doorways but also surround a large fireplace.

ABOVE This tall wall, comprising carefully placed random-size stones, affords total privacy. The gate opens to a water view; stone plant beds add contrasting shapes and colors.

ABOVE RIGHT Completing an idyllic lakeside setting, stone forms a generous outdoor dining room plus a grand fireplace topped by a traditional chimney.

RIGHT A raised fireplace framed in gleaming steel is set into a smoothly crafted stone wall to make a perfect setting for intimate evening gatherings.

ABOVE The cartouche on this fireplace looks hand-carved but is really the result of the scagliola process. First developed in 17th century Italy, this blend of crushed marble, limestone, and travertine is hand-molded rather than chiseled.

ABOVE RIGHT Hand-carved filigree adds a dimension of style to the stone facade of a 19th-century town house.

RIGHT An elegant transition from the outside of the house to its glass-enclosed interior, this stone-wrapped plant bed is a platform for an ever-changing array of ornamental flowers and greenery.

OPPOSITE Contrasting shapes and tones give character to this stately columned veranda. The floor comprises large slate tiles; the walls and column bases are random-cut stones with a fresh-from-the-quarry rough surface.

chunks, slabs, and ornamentation

Step on it. Whether individual pieces shaped by nature are set on the ground to form a footpath or carefully cut units are arranged in a planned pattern, stone is a natural choice when producing a surface on which to walk. It's hardy, unaffected by weather, and resilient. Stone can be manipulated to create varying shapes and finishes, but all tonal differences are achieved in nature: high temperatures and varying pressures under the earth's surface act on different minerals to create the stone colors, for unparalled variations.

walkways

ABOVE FAR LEFT Bluestone squares and rectangles in varied sizes are joined like puzzle pieces to form the straight edges of a walk that leads to an open patio.

ABOVE LEFT Pink sandstone pavers are tightly mortared to create a smooth surface underfoot. Slight color variations lend character to this flower-trimmed patio.

ABOVE Hand-set river stones were used on the outer walls and the retaining wall of this contemporary home. Stones cut in random shapes form the walkway and stairs with their machine-cut stone borders.

LEFT Naturally shaped stones were hand picked to create this curving garden path, a transition from a house to the wide lawn beyond it.

OPPOSITE Stone steps, as if placed by nature, lead to a white-painted hilltop pergola. Pebbles fill gaps between the stones, discouraging weed growth along the rising path.

artistic landscapes

LEFT Bluestone tops the stone entry that leads to wide grass and gracefully curving bluestone steps, connecting the upper and lower segments of a land-scaped backyard.

RIGHT Stones in mixed shapes and sizes are arranged informally to fashion a path pointing to a backyard garden and running stream.

sizes and **s**hapes

Machines make the difference. These pebbles and stones look as though they are lifted from an active river bed and shaped over thousands of years. The examples, below, in different color and shape variations, were produced by steel blades, then honed to create smooth surfaces. When used decoratively, honed surfaces are more porous and less vividly colored than polished stone, which is so smooth it's rarely used outdoors.

LEFT Flagstone steps set into granite walls rise in stages to a sun-lit lawn enveloped by 100-year-old trees.

OPPOSITE Artistically shaped, flagstones and lines of brick create a patio that has an outdoor fireplace. River rock was was also used decoratively on the base of the stucco walls.

coloration

Sandstone has been used extensively in buildings for over 100 years because of its uniform texture. Below, stone samples in yellow-brown and yellow-pink with natural cleft surfaces show the possibilities of using various colors and tones for an appealing look.

ABOVE Nearly matched bluestones form a wide walkway with a flush cobblestone edge. The walk splits in two directions, forming a perfect "T."

RIGHT To add texture and interest to this widening in a stone path embraced by a garden of succulents, a freeform trickle of blue dyed pebbles flows from one end to the other.

Whether you're surfacing a kitchen floor or a countertop, stone is a likely choice because of its versatility and rich coloration. Stone floors are cut tiles that are grouted together for a smooth surface.

kitchen cavalcade

Any type of countertop edge treatment is possible, even with the hardest stone. Stone countertops are crafted from slabs—usually in 5 x 8-foot sizes. For counters or island surfaces longer than 8 feet, seams are required. But skilled fabricators can abut adjoining slabs and grout them so effectively that the seams seem virtually invisible.

ABOVE A raised granite counter provides multiple meal-prep and eating stations around a central sink and range in this open kitchen. The height and configuration of the counter provide a subtle separation between the principal cook and any diners and relatives or friends helping to get food to the table.

LEFT Fieldstone walls frame three sets of French doors that link this huge kitchen to the stone patio outdoors. The two-level granite countertop has a slightly curved pencil edge.

OPPOSITE The range hood in this soaring, symmetrical kitchen is embellished with scagliola stone, a hand-formed process that had its origins in late-Renaissance Italy. The stone flooring is in a herring-bone pattern. The countertops, except for the island, are granite with a custom edge.

OPPOSITE FAR LEFT Cast-stone ornamentation with botanical imagery borders a warm-toned stone counter.

▌

OPPOSITE LEFT Steel rods that mimic the dishwasher handle are embedded in a sloping granite countertop. The rods also hold hot pots; the sloping section acts as a drainboard, so spilled water can flow into the undermount sink.

▌

OPPOSITE BOTTOM A slab of black granite, angled at the mitered corners, provides a lowered breakfast bar at one end of the granite-topped island in this kitchen. The island extends around a tempered-glass cooktop set into the stone, designed as the kitchen's centerpiece.

▌

RIGHT An exhaust hood is hidden behind ornamented scagliola stone. This hand-formed process combines techniques used in creating both cast and cut stone. Countertops around the range and stainless-steel undermount sink are granite with straight edges.

▌

BELOW The main counters in this kitchen are glazed lava stone, a natural product quarried in the south of France. Gray is only one of a range of available colors, all of which are produced in a high-sheen finish.

edge **o**ptions

When you are choosing an edge treatment, one of the things to consider is the style of your kitchen. You will want this important finishing detail to complement the room's overall look. However, slab thickness will ultimately determine what edge choices are possible.

For a thin stone countertop, a straight edge is the usual choice, although it may be possible to have a radius edge, which has a slight curve at the top. Thicker stone surfaces allow you to choose one of these more common edge treatments:

▌ **Bevel**—a slight angle in the top 35 percent of an edge.
▌ **Bullnose**—an edge carved into the shape of a half-circle.
▌ **Half Bullnose**—an edge with a sweeping curve, like a quarter-circle.
▌ **Pencil**—a nearly straight edge but with a less pronounced curve.
▌ **Stepped Bullnose**—a standard bullnose with a notch at the top.
▌ **Ogee**—a truly elegant edge, shaped like an elongated "S" curve.

The bathroom is where natural stone in many of its forms and finishes is used lavishly for both a dramatic and practical effect—on walls, floors, sinks, counters, and often even on tubs. Whether a hard granite is selected or a softer, more porous marble or limestone, natural stone makes a strong statement—in its veining and its color variations. Found in nature—in ancient and new quarries in various parts of the world—stone presents an uneven image, as no two pieces are ever exactly alike. For many people, these differences and apparent imperfections only add to its appeal. These bathroom fixtures, all made from natural stone, can inspire you. With the limitless ways of handling stone, perhaps you will dream up your own design for a very individual custom order.

bath bonanza

ABOVE Perfect for powder rooms or well-appointed guest baths, these exquisitely veined vessel-style sinks, carved from the thinnest onyx, have a rich translucence that makes them seem to shimmer in any kind of light.

BELOW Carved from a single stone slab, this giant tub with gently tapered sides and a sculpted edge and base dominates a bathroom where stone floor tiles are set in a diamond pattern with contrasting inset squares.

OPPOSITE Dark blue with a tall, elongated cutout, a wall of Venetian plaster separates the tapered wood vanity from the rest of a lavish contemporary-style bath. The floor, of cast catera stone with myriad flaws providing character and interest, unites the entire space.

LEFT The chiaroscuro of black and white in this iron washbasin stand and vessel sink evoke a period gone by but have beautifully simple lines. The counter is generously sized to accommodate the large-diameter onyx bowl.

ABOVE RIGHT This vessel-style sink is carved from pure white stone, flawlessly curved on the outside with a similarly curved interior and a flattened rim.

BELOW In this sleek bathroom setting, the walls are stone, as is the vanity. The sink is sunk into slabs of cut stone that appear to rest on open shelving. The countertop slabs are secured at both ends, and the tub is sunk into a platform of cast stone. Each stone component has been carved by diamond blades for precision.

care giving

For longevity, stone should be protected with a penetrating sealer, applied before initial use and periodically thereafter. Floors should be swept regularly, then mopped with a solution of mild detergent and water; after a warm-water rinse, the surface should be allowed to dry thoroughly to prevent streaking. Waxing any stone floor will produce a perilously slippery surface.

Avoid using bleach, vinegar, or ammonia, and never rub on abrasive cleansers. Mop up or sponge off spills as soon as possible to prevent the possibility of permanent staining. Rust spots can be challenging, particularly on surfaces that may be somewhat porous. First, purchase a commercial rust remover formulated for the type of stone that's been stained. Then, mixed with an equal amount of powdered whiting, or talc chalk, apply it to the stain. You may need to leave this mixture on the spot for two full days before the rust vanishes.

ABOVE This sink, carved into a wide, sweeping shape, shows none of the veining so often associated with granite. It's been honed to achieve a soft, non-glossy sheen. As the honing process opens pores in stone, the periodic protection of a spray-on sealer is needed.

LEFT Lined with 16-gauge double-walled copper that has been fused into a moderately elongated stone shell, this vessel-style sink is likely to acquire an even richer appearance over time. With the passing years, the copper liner will develop a weathered patina, adding measurably to the sink's timeless appeal.

ABOVE LEFT A bathtub that gleams in sunlight pouring through a stationary window made of clear acrylic blocks is set into a stone platform.

▮

ABOVE A pedestal sink that recalls vintage washstands, this wide, circular onyx bowl mounted on an iron stand was delicately machine-carved to achieve a degree of thinnes that approaches translucency.

▮

LEFT In this European-style open bathroom, the shower, vanity, and walls are a composite of mixed stone. This large space has a single drain in the sloping floor to catch any water. Open circles in the shower partition are echoed in motifs cut into the stone floor.

RIGHT This custom variation on the traditional console has a rectangular stone sink set onto two pairs of stainless-steel legs. The sink is perfectly positioned against the 12 x 12-in. marble tiles that comprise the floor and wall.

BELOW Imported Italian marble on the floor and back wall and rough-surfaced stone artistically embedded with shells create this unusual shower. Illumination comes from the openings in the custom-made pottery wall lights.

BELOW RIGHT In this detail of the vanity shown on page 82 (opposite bottom), it's possible to see that the sink was carved out of a single stone square. The bowl's precise shape is the result of 21st-century machine tooling.

bright idea

spot test

To check the porosity of any stone, obtain an unsealed sample and let water stand on it for 10 minutes. If the surface wipes clean, it's nonporous; if there's a ring, it's porous.

OPPOSITE TOP FAR LEFT Carved from a single slab of stone, this custom-size columnar sink has classical leaf motifs chiseled into the sides and base.

OPPOSITE TOP RIGHT An oversize pedestal sink with a deeply incised exterior has a semispherical shape so that it fits flush against the wall.

OPPOSITE A stainless-steel vessel-style sink is mounted in the center of an onyx slab that serves as a countertop at the end of an all-white bathroom.

ABOVE Polished smooth and shiny within a rough-textured bowl, this blue granite vessel rests on a wood counter.

ABOVE RIGHT A custom-designed vessel sink is set in what was cast to resemble the base of a Corinthian column.

RIGHT The walls and floor of this cutting-edge master bath are 12 x 12-in. catera stone tiles. The crescent-shaped counter from the same material is cut and shaped from a single slab.

No decorating element rivals the warmth of a working fireplace. Once a home's sole heat source, a fireplace is now an accent, even in homes with more than one. There was a time when brick

hearth dreams

was a fireplace staple; now, natural stones are in wide use. With today's new direct-vent and vent-free units, chimneys are unnecessary. Fireplaces can be located on any walls: not only in living and family rooms but also in bedrooms, kitchens, and even bathrooms. Think of a fireplace as eye comfort: a source of visual as well as physical warmth.

For a rustic look, there are fireplaces made of rough-surfaced, random-shaped stones. For refined elegance, there are stone units with hand-carved trim. With its classic veining and variable finish, stone can add texture and interest to any design. Each of these fireplaces exemplifies the beauty of natural stone as well as its strength and durability.

ABOVE Different-sized stones, hunted and collected, were cemented together to create the face of this majestic fireplace in a weekend home in the woods.

RIGHT A more refined use of stones, each individually cut, was picked to create a fireplace and chimney that rise through the center of a large, open kitchen.

OPPOSITE What appears to be a random pile of slabs and stones is actually a carefully planned fireplace beside a large firewood niche. The rustic nature of this configuration is achieved by mixing stone shapes, sizes, and colors.

the fireplace as an inevitable focus

ABOVE LEFT In this lodge-like family room with a tall tray ceiling, the arch of the stone fireplace opening mimics the huge arched window that dominates one wall of the room.

ABOVE A raised fireplace made of smooth river-washed stones is the centerpiece of the sitting area in the great room of a large suburban home.

LEFT Arranged row upon row, the square tiles applied to this fireplace vary in size, and some have incised motifs. In an unusual juxtaposition, the painted wood mantel is traditional in style.

OPPOSITE Creating a decorating focus, the floor-level fireplace in this contemporary living room rises to ceiling height. The firebox itself is clearly lined with fireproof brick.

RIGHT In an outdoor kitchen with a cooking hearth, the grill and cooktop fit in the niche, along with a built-in dishwasher. Rough-cut stones form the exterior; smooth stone tiles line the inner wall.

BELOW Caught in the beams of track lighting, a steel mantel provides sleek contrast to the random-size stones that form this tall family-room fireplace. The stones are cemented in place with no grouting.

OPPOSITE A slab of solid slate is the surface of the coffee table in this wood-paneled living room. The stone fireplace has two same-shape openings: the larger one is for the firebox; the smaller, for log storage.

do's and don'ts

A fireplace makes a strong architectural statement in any room. The following guidelines will help you make the most of this important design element.

▌ **DO** think of a fireplace as eye comfort, a source of visual as well as physical warmth.

▌ **DON'T** neglect scale when planning a fireplace. Oversized, it can visually overwhelm a room; undersized, it's likely to make a room feel less important.

▌ **DO** consider the mood you want for the room while deciding on the color and texture of the stones when choosing a fireplace style.

▌ **DON'T** settle for a basic "builder box." For a true focal-point fireplace, visit a showroom with a variety of styles.

▌ **DO** have the firebox lined with fireproof brick.

▌ **DON'T** rely entirely on samples; select the actual stones that will be used to build your fireplace, no matter where you plan to place it in your home.

▌ **DO** keep in mind how the fireplace will look in warm weather, when there's no fire or flame. Andirons, an ornamental screen, or a decorated mantel will hold the focus.

▌ **DON'T** forget to have a penetrating sealer applied to any natural stone that frames the fireplace. That's the surest way to prevent possible staining from ashes or soot.

LEFT There is a slate ledge at the base of this raised fireplace, a gas-fed unit with its own heat-resistant steel firebox. This is a vent-free unit, with a catalytic con-verter that precludes the necessity of providing any exhaust outlet.

BELOW The off-center chimney of this stone fireplace adds decorating impact to a light-filled room.

OPPOSITE The chimney is a steel tube, and the wall behind it is glass block. It's the contrasting materials that give this stone fireplace its prominence and drama. On the dining area wall is a framed piece of art made from stone embedded with an ancient fossil.

Just as sculptors, for centuries, have found that marble, granite, and other richly veined types of stone are appealing to work, modern-day artisans consider stone a practical and attractive material for creating decorative products. Whether hand-carved and finished by the stonecutter or a design interpreted by mechanical means, each piece is unique. Shelving, tables, benches, platters, and bowls—all have felt the touch of the stone artist.

refinements

TOP LEFT Heavy and virtually indestructible, this set of stone bowls is designed for everyday use. The scooped-out interiors have the low-level sheen of a honed surface.

ABOVE Elegant modern pottery is arranged on a freeform shelf cut from 1,000-year-old stone that rests on a wall-mounted wood support.

MIDDLE LEFT Pale but hardy, these serving bowls were each carved from individual chunks of honey onyx.

BOTTOM LEFT The subtle curve of this slate serving plate results from the skillful application of sculpting tools. Properly sealed platters like this one resist food stains and are usually left unharmed by residential dishwashers.

the usual finishes

▌ **Acid-washed:** An acidic material creates an aged or textured look.

▌ **Brushed:** Applying a coarse wire brush smoothes the surface and results in a time-worn finish.

▌ **Flamed:** The process involves high heat to produce an unrefined, exceedingly rough texture.

▌ **Honed:** A machine is used to achieve a smooth, satiny surface with a flat, or matte, appearance.

▌ **Pillowed:** This is a method that slightly rounds the edges of stone tiles, for a pillow-like effect.

▌ **Polished:** Another machine process, it draws out the deepest stone colors and yields the shiniest surfaces.

▌ **Tumbled:** Stone can be placed in a tumbling drum along with pebbles and chemicals for a worn effect.

ABOVE Mounted on a wood base, this solid granite tabletop has the rough edging that attests to the handwork that produced its unique configuration. Most of its top surface is highly polished; the chiseled-out lower level is honed. Within the square, as in a carefully orchestrated Japanese garden, are small river rocks in water.

▌

LEFT A contemporary product that recalls ancient artistry, this granite bench is a marriage of elements, each carved by hand from a single raw chunk. The legs are rough-cut blocks, and the seat has a completely smooth surface despite its roughened edges. "Elegant simplicity" is how the fabricator describes it. Although often used as interior accents, stone benches are at home outdoors if frequently resealed for protection from the elements.

3

Thrust into the earth's crust by millennia of volcanic rumblings deep beneath the surface, granite is a hardened mix of igneous rock and a great pastiche of crystalline minerals. Quarried in various parts of the world, it is sometimes found in outcroppings enveloped by patches of flat, sandy soil; other times it is extracted from boulders dug out of mountain canyons. Mineral content determines granite's colors, all of which occur in nature. Despite radical differences in color and graining, all granites share common traits of strength and solidity, making them a practical choice for a variety of domestic uses.

Take it for Granite

▌beauty and versatility ▌
▌kitchen options ▌ bath digs ▌

Two different granites, each with its own edge treatment, point up the versatility of this surface material in a kitchen where a shaped island has a spherical sink cutout.

Granite's enviable toughness and wide availability have made it the stone of choice in key residential as well as commercial applications. Because its hardy surface almost defies weather damage, it has long been used to create the distinguished face of office buildings worldwide. Now it appears domestically in nearly every room of the house: on floors, walls, stairways, the facades of fireplaces, and the tops of counters, where it remains amazingly undamaged by either kitchen knives or hot pots. There is elegance in its tone and texture, and its long-term durability is awesome. A gift from the ages, granite can withstand a lifetime of abuse. In any form, it is a most forgiving product.

beauty and versatility

LEFT Corinthian granite stones plus a slab of polished granite add up to a fireplace that separates a family room and kitchen. Wood storage is behind a small side door.

ABOVE Polished granite tiles, installed tightly to resemble a single slab, encase this living room door in a highly reflective surface.

BELOW The frame and risers of a stairway leading to a media room are faced with tiles installed, like those above, to resemble a single polished granite slab.

OPPOSITE Shaped granite treads and risers form a sleek staircase in a home with Art Deco accoutrements.

ranite is as hardy as your kitchen's heaviest iron frypan. It resists nicks, scratches, and scorching, and its beauty is legendary. Some granites are porous, however; they must be dutifully sealed, and when used on the floor they can be slippery when wet. A range of finishes would enable you to easily adapt this stone to any home need. *Polished* is a high-gloss finish that makes a particularly powerful color statement. *Brushed* creates a smooth surface with a timeless, worn character. *Flamed,* ideal for floors, is roughened, the result of high heat. *Honed* presents a smooth-as-satin finish with a flat rather than reflective look.

kitchen
options

TOP In a partial redo of an existing kitchen, a new countertop was installed directly over an existing surface, creating an easy transformation from old and worn to sparkling new. What looks like a granite slab cut to accommodate two undermount sinks is actually a series of tiles pressed so close together that the grout is virtually invisible.

ABOVE, RIGHT, AND OPPOSITE Despite the hazards of existing columns and beams, none of which could be moved or eliminated, the owners of a city apartment merged two small rooms into a spacious kitchen-dining space. Granite counters reflect natural sunlight, ceiling lights, and the high-intensity task lighting supplied by an arrangement of pendant fixtures.

IIIIIII computerized cuts and edge treatments IIIIIIIIIII

OPPOSITE AND ABOVE In redoing her kitchen, the owner told her designer. "All I want is a classic white kitchen." What she got was a white-painted bead-board backsplash, white recessed-panel cabinets, and white ogee-edged granite countertops.

ABOVE RIGHT In what appears a seamless granite installation, this kitchen countertop was created from tightly placed tiles placed directly over an existing surface—another quick and easy transformation.

RIGHT Granite with a large ogee edge tops an island that has cupboards and drawers on two sides. The countertop, cut from one stone slab, extends over classic pilasters at the corners.

LEFT Black granite counters plus brushed nickel fittings and cabinet hardware lend understated elegance to this contemporary kitchen.

BELOW Poor light and layout, with too little storage and workspace, prompted a professional chef to add windows to his own kitchen and remove some interior walls. He chose black granite to top twin islands.

OPPOSITE TOP The owners of a Mediterranean-style home absorbed a seldom-used room into the kitchen, then set a granite island into the arch between the expanded kitchen and dining room.

OPPOSITE BOTTOM Adding a sculptural shape to the geometry of this remodeled space, a custom-designed range hood spills light onto a cooktop set into a Black Absolute granite surface, which also forms the backsplash.

fast fixes

Recently imported materials now make it possible to have the look plus the indestructible surface of granite without doing a major demolition.

- **You can transform** almost any surface by the application of special tiles over whatever material you have. These tiles are set so close together that the result resembles a single slab of granite.
- **The beauty** of such transformations is that change can occur quickly, so you can enjoy the benefits shared by all users of granite. If the work is done skillfully, no one need know that yours is not a complete kitchen makeover.

OPPOSITE AND BELOW In a splash of versatility, this granite countertop has roughened irregularity on its forward edge and on the top edge of the backsplash.

ABOVE AND RIGHT A rare form of granite with dramatic marble-like veining is used on counters and backsplashes, and as trim around this kitchen's single window. Note that at the far end of the island (above), granite in a freeform shape panels parts of two sides of an angled wall.

ABOVE RIGHT In a remodeled kitchen with tile walls and flooring, the granite countertop flanks a pure-white farm sink.

LEFT How effectively granite can be used with other stone products is shown in a kitchen where a black crushed-granite counter is offset by a tumbled-marble backsplash.

OPPOSITE Dramatic contrasts mark the use of granite in this designer kitchen, where texture shares the spotlight with tone. Multi-dimensional edge treatments add refinement to a room that combines traditional style with contemporary functionality.

BELOW A sweeping boomerang-shaped counter on two levels is another example of an easy transformation. Tiles tightly installed to resemble seamless granite slabs are applied to an existing surface for an entirely new look.

For pampering the senses, few materials are as inviting as granite, with its rich textures, dramatic veining, and color choices that literally stretch the palette. Granite's expanding popularity is astonishing, as so many synthetic alternatives are available today. But it is clear that granite's appeal is largely because it is a natural product that was formed when fiery magma near the earth's core merged with feldspar, quartz, mica, and other minerals to create unique textures and coloration. In the bath, specifically on countertops, the sheen of polished granite is highly desirable, presenting a finish nearly as sleek and reflective as a bathroom mirror. Under foot, granite in a roughened finish creates a tough surface that is slip-proof, wet or dry. For the people who love it, granite is a safe bet and best used in the bath.

bath digs

OPPOSITE Like a giant vessel sink, a soaking tub in granite—rough on the outside but polished smooth on the inside—dominates a bathroom where the countertop is a slightly shaped granite slab.

TOP Each component of this pedestal sink is carved from a single chunk of black granite. Fused together, the elements comprise an elegant fixture, especially the sink, which has the hand-shaped look of sculpture.

ABOVE To shoehorn a larger tub into a relatively small bath without going to the trouble of knocking down walls, the homeowners opted to angle the tub, framing it with a deck and steps topped with granite.

ABOVE AND RIGHT A custom arrangement of exotic Costa Esmerelda granite tiles mixed with porcelain and copper-blend tiles gives these tub and shower areas a special look.

ABOVE RIGHT AND OPPOSITE For a bathroom with a mountain view, the designer devised a stone design that mimics the landscape the homeowners oversee. The "torn stone" is highly polished—along with the mirrored wall above it, and reflects the opposite window wall.

BELOW A pair of porcelain sinks is mounted atop a counter made of closely set tiles that resemble a single slab of granite.

how to keep it looking great

▌ **For countertops** in food preparation areas, make sure your installer applies a nontoxic penetrating sealer. It will make the surface spill-resistant and ensure that you can cut on it.

▌ **For everyday counter cleanups,** use a sponge or soft cloth with a mild liquid dish detergent mixed with warm water, then rinse.

▌ **For granite floors,** no matter what the finish, dust with a fresh, nontreated dust mop. When necessary, clean with a mop soaked in a solution of mild household cleaner and warm water.

▌ **For any granite surface,** avoid grout, tub, or tile cleaners with acid. And never use abrasive cleaners or harsh cleaning implements.

bright idea

precaution!

Though durable, granite is porous. Some granites stain easily and should be sealed after installation, then sealed yearly, depending on frequency of use.

OPPOSITE Trimmed in wood, this rectangular granite backsplash and countertop in a marble-like pattern is topped by a mirror that reflects a frameless glass shower and makes a narrow bathroom feel considerably larger.

RIGHT Distressed cherry cabinetry adds a period touch to a sumptuous powder room where a painted-floral sink is set into a granite counter.

BELOW A stall shower received a modest makeover when resurfaced in tiles installed to resemble ceiling-high slabs of granite to create a glamorous master bath.

arble is a luminous material that, since antiquity, has been quarried all over the world. It's a metamorphic rock that achieves its character from contact with sedimentary rock such as limestone. The swirls and veins of many strains of marble result from impurities—clay, sand, silt, and iron oxides among them. All create a recrystallization caused by the pressure and heat underground. Marble is relatively soft compared with other natural stone products, but its tensile strength makes it unlikely to shatter. Its characteristic glow results from light penetrating beneath the surface, creating a sleek, waxy look.

Marble Opportunity

▌ glowing beauty ▌
▌ kitchens with caution ▌
▌ bath gems ▌

Adding to the exotic nature of this pool, local stones, shells, and rocks form a wall, while African marble tiles form stepping-stones that appear to float across the pool.

Over time, marble has attained its status as the most elegant of nature's bounty. Like granite, with which it's often compared, marble is available in a wide range of dazzling colors. Because marble is sold in two basic grades—commercial and select—it's possible to know in advance the quality of whatever you prefer. Select marble is more costly; it also has fewer imperfections. Because of its inherent softness, it can be beautifully

glowing beauty

handcrafted to suit individual needs and a variety of styles. Fireplace design is a popular marble application, and modern artisans have become adept at re-creating classic architectural forms to give their designs timeless focus. Depending on how or where it's used, marble can reflect the past in authentic-style reproductions or present itself in a contemporary way, but as one designer describes it, marble "has an eternal feel."

ABOVE Adapted from a design by Thomas Hope, an eighteenth-century English collector of marble sculptures and decorative works, this fireplace design, with its tapering pilasters, shows Egyptian influence, even though it easily suits a contemporary setting.

LEFT A wall of marble tiles centered around a massive fireplace gives this two-story-high windowed living room its focus and drama. Marble tiles come in many thicknesses, and can be cut to tiles of any size or shape.

OPPOSITE This detailed white marble reproduction, a design inspired by the work of the eighteenth-century English architect William Chambers, has fluted pilasters topped by ionic capitals. The central frieze boasts a hand-carved urn and foliage. Framing the fireplace opening are bands of brilliantly colored Siena marble, which add a new dimension of style to the classic design.

ABOVE Hand-carved
rosettes top twin pilasters of
this white marble fireplace.
They are carved and reeded
with diagonal ribbons, and
the reeding continues along
the edge of the mantel.

OPPOSITE Framing an
arched fireplace opening,
this Victorian reproduction
in white marble adds height
to counter the tall arched
window. Two massive cor-
bels support a reeded mantel, adding elegance to this
formal dining room.

RIGHT A timeless Italian
design in a soft earth tone,
this fireplace would be as
strong a presence in an elegantly cluttered country
house as in this simple,
stark setting. Here, a gilded
mirror adds a traditional element to this room's spare
contemporary furnishings.

OPPOSITE Curves dominate this fireplace, derived from a period French design that shows off the skills of artisans who find marble an easily workable and forgiving medium.

LEFT Curvaceous and uncluttered, this modern take on an early eighteenth-century Queen Anne-style fireplace would be at home in any setting.

BELOW LEFT A sign of welcome in an English country house, this copy of a mid-eighteenth-century fireplace supplies visual and actual warmth.

BELOW With fluted ionic columns and an entablature adorned with classical urns and a ewer, this reproduction of a period chimneypiece is an homage to the Scottish architect Robert Adam.

| | | | | | | | | | reproductions with elegance and style | | | | | | | | | | | |

Marble creates a surface that always commands attention, but in a kitchen it also demands attention. Here it works best where it's less likely to be subjected to cuts and spills—a baking center, for example, where its cool smoothness is ripe for kneading and rolling dough. In a workhorse area, care must be taken to wipe up spills immediately—particularly from tomatoes and other acidic juices—to avoid permanent staining. A protective penetrating sealer, applied regularly by a professional, will ensure marble's long life, and using cutting boards will prevent nicks and scratches from chopping and slicing. Marble can be marvelous when handled with care.

kitchens with caution

OPPOSITE Marble takes center stage in this remodeled eat-in kitchen, which has up-to-date amenities. Reinforcing the 1930's design statement, white 3 x 5-in. ceramic tiles create a backsplash.

ABOVE Sweeping curves cut into a marble countertop accentuate the elegance of a double undermount porcelain sink.

RIGHT A gold-plated towel bar frames countertops fabricated from Calcutta Gold marble, which is warm white and accented with gold, gray and taupe veining. The tall vases are marble obelisks.

BELOW White marble used throughout this remodeled kitchen adds crispness and contrast to a setting designed for homeowners who love to cook.

TOP A favorite family and guest gathering spot, the marble-topped island separates a kitchen from the adjacent dining area. It's where everyone comes together to watch the homeowners, two talented cooks, prepare special meals.

ABOVE Gray marble complements the gleam of stainless-steel undermount sinks set into a countertop that extends along a sun-lit window wall of a remodeled kitchen.

RIGHT Glass mosaic tiles form cabinet-high backsplashes behind peripheral black marble counters in a completely remodeled condominium kitchen. The kitchen's centerpiece—widened by a notched-out "L" to make room for breakfast and snack dining—is a long, wide island that includes a drop-in vegetable sink and six-burner cooktop.

bath gems

t is in bathrooms where marble really shines, and particularly in guest baths and powder rooms, where homeowners are likely to tap into marble's panoply of vast colors and sophisticated patterns.

In any bath, marble maintenance should occur regularly, to keep the surface looking bright and flawless. Soap scum is the foremost bathroom maintenance issue. Keeping a squeegee handy (and using it often) is one way to expunge the problem, but should scum buildup occur, the best way to remove it is with a packaged soap-scum remover or a solution of a half-cup of ammonia to a full gallon of water. Be sure to mix with care. Over-use of ammonia can eventually dull even the brightest marble surface.

OPPOSITE Large-scale marble tiles, mounted tightly together like a vast, vertical checkerboard, comprise an open shower in a remodeled master bathroom. The antique, lacquered-wood armchair adds spa-like comfort and a gracious period touch.

ABOVE A uniquely fabricated glass vessel-style sink is mounted atop a marble counter with the color and texture of polished wood. Color intensity creates a dramatic contrast offset by the neutral tone of the brushed-nickel faucet.

RIGHT Like an in-house grotto that presents many colors, this curtainless step-in shower—with back and upper walls of imported marble cut into tiles and side walls of rough-carved local stones with inset seashells—has niches for soaps and shampoos. Windows of tempered glass afford privacy without impeding the input of natural light.

bright idea

wax it!

Periodic applications of paste wax will maintain marble's natural sheen, which can be dulled by frequent cleanings.

LEFT With its sculptural shape and subtly veined white coloration, this marble tub is deep enough for one to enjoy a generous soak and long enough for two to share a lavish bathing experience.

BOTTOM LEFT Ogee-edged marble tops a vanity in a glamorous master bath with cabinets in the same gray color.

BELOW Undermount sinks are suspended beneath oval openings cut into the marble countertop. Exposed pipes, used as towel bars, are polished steel.

OPPOSITE The curving, heavily veined counter appears to float in a bathroom lit by softly filtered sconces installed near ceiling height.

LEFT Soft and feminine was the goal when designing a woman's bath where a frameless shower is lined with pink marble.

BELOW Like an island of opulence, this step-up marble tub deck is crafted around two structural piers in a windowed master bath. The black-and-gold armchair stands beside the stall shower, which is pictured on page 128.

OPPOSITE TOP Blue-veined marble complements the pale wood paneling in this custom master bath designed with classic style.

OPPOSITE BOTTOM LEFT Peach-colored marble, with a gently curving forward edge, tops an antique wood cabinet that serves as this powder room's vanity.

OPPOSITE BOTTOM RIGHT Shiny white marble wraps a compact-size bathroom in brilliance. Bright light and reflective surfaces make the room feel infinitely bigger.

I I I I I I I I I I I I classic looks in contemporary colors I I I I I I I I I I I I

Limestone is a sedimentary rock made mainly from calcium carbonate, a mineral that crystallizes in seawater or is formed from the underwater accumulation of shells plus tiny organisms. Waves break down these particles into fragments that, compacted with sand, mud, and clay, harden to form limestone. Travertine, a variety of limestone formed from minerals that dissolve in underground springs, is delivered to the earth's surface by rivers, springs, and geysers. Each of these materials is white, like chalk (a type of limestone), but carbon and iron oxide create the products' surprising colors.

Texture Terrain

‖ surface stunners ‖ creative kitchens ‖
‖ bathing beauty ‖ outdoor splash ‖

A spacious dressing room is reflected in a mirrored wall of a glassed-in limestone bathroom. This modern jewel-box design embraces the Southwestern landscape.

Limestone is amazingly long lasting. In ancient times it was used to construct Egypt's fabled pyramids, just as Rome's coliseum was built of travertine. Just as sleek and glamorous as marble, polished limestone can be slippery, which is why a honed finish

surface stunners

is generally recommended for flooring. Limestone and travertine are known as freestones. With no preferred direction for splitting, each can be cut and carved into any desired configuration. Whether machine-sawed or hand-worked, it can answer the needs of the most demanding designs.

ABOVE Seemingly endless limestone flooring unites the separate functions of an expansive kitchen-dining room. With few interior walls, this house is a fabulous example of open-space living.

LEFT Hardwood planks installed diagonally in a corner define a home office located in a large entry hall where the floor is otherwise topped with travertine. The two surfaces meet at dynamic angles that create an eye-catching ziggurat shape.

OPPOSITE In a lavish Southern California home, gray-and-cream-colored French limestone in a diamond pattern draws the eye from the two-story entrance hall through an arched opening into the living room at the rear of the house.

OPPOSITE Brushed steel plus three different stones, including limestone, comprise this contemporary fireplace and mantel. The fireplace is raised slightly, allowing room for a floor-level drawer for ash removal.

ABOVE The designer of this limestone fireplace calls it "The Totem," a reflection of the abstract shapes of the two pilasters that seem to support the chest-high mantel.

ABOVE RIGHT Like a giant picture frame, this custom limestone fireplace has an inner frame of steel, which makes it even more suitable for a contemporary setting.

RIGHT French limestone was used to create this stunningly simple raised fireplace with a niche for decorative objects.

pros can pull it all together

Flawless installation is the ultimate key to the appearance and functionality of any stone surface.

❚ **Interview** at least three candidates, requesting references and learning how much experience each installer has had handling your particular choice of stone.

❚ **Insist on** receiving bids in writing that include the cost of the materials and labor needed to prepare the surface as well as fabrication and installation of the product itself.

❚ **To prevent complications** down the road—in case problems arise or an accident occurs at the site—make sure your installer is licensed and insured.

Travertine in its natural state is pocked by tiny holes that are often factory-filled with stone-dust resin to achieve smoothness. Limestone surfaces are extraordinarily smooth, with a velvet-like finish. Both materials will complement any other surface in a kitchen design, whether it's the cloudy sheen of tempered glass, the gloss of limestone or travertine, the cool grayness of stainless steel, or the rich texture of grained wood. Where floors and countertops are concerned, the toughest stone varieties are recommended, but even they must be sealed to protect against stains and spills. What threatens the long, serviceable life of limestone and travertine the most are knives, acidic liquids, and neglect.

creative kitchens

TOP AND RIGHT An arrangement of 14-in.-sq. limestone tiles creates a softly colored floor in a giant U-shaped kitchen with stainless-steel appliances set into pale wood cabinets topped with shiny black granite counters. A raised tempered-glass breakfast bar, designed with a sweeping curve, appears to float over one side of the elongated work island. Shelving in a wide adjacent doorway puts a few of the homeowners' collectibles on display.

ABOVE Varicolored limestone tiles add an earthy touch to a large kitchen with built-in appliances and custom cabinetry in three types of wood. Sunlight pouring in through a skylight in the center of the space complements the sophisticated indirect lighting.

LEFT Shown at the conclusion of an extensive remodeling, this Newport Beach, California, kitchen presents an agreeable mix of elements: stainless-steel built-in appliances, granite countertops, and a shallow backsplash, plus limestone flooring—tiles set on the diagonal.

RIGHT A giant farm sink is set between sets of recessed-panel wood cabinets topped with ogee-edged limestone counters.

BELOW Travertine flooring unifies the spaces in this remodeled eat-in kitchen, the pale tone offsetting the cabinet's warm wood.

handle with care

Limestone and travertine require routine maintenance:

- **DO** dust-mop limestone and travertine floors regularly, and blot up spills as soon as possible.
- **DON'T** apply tub, tile, or grout cleaner or any cleaning product whose label indicates that it contains acid.
- **DO** clean surfaces with a mild solution of liquid detergent and warm water.
- **DON'T** use any abrasive cleaners, rough sponges, brushes, or scouring pads.
- **DO** protect tabletops with coasters, trivets, and place-mats; flooring, with area rugs on top of nonslip mats.
- **DON'T** forget to apply a penetrating sealer to shield the surface. In food-preparation and dining areas, be sure that sealer is labeled nontoxic.

bathing beauty

A bathroom can be an ideal showcase for the use of natural stone such as travertine or limestone. Here, there is less likelihood of damage from knife cuts and acid spills. Except on the floor—where a polished surface would not be a good idea—sheen and sparkle are welcome. While it is true that no two stones are alike, it's possible to maximize the visual impact of the materials you choose by juxtaposing slabs or tiles in slightly different colors and patterns. Contrast can be a dynamic gift of nature.

OPPOSITE Limestone tiles are installed throughout this spacious bathroom. Seen on the tub deck, on walls (including those of the semi-open shower), and on the floor, the large squares are separated by bands of limestone in a contrasting tone.

TOP Filled travertine—a surface made exceptionally smooth when its tiny holes are packed with stone-dust resin—was used on the walls and the spherical step-up tub deck in this master bathroom.

ABOVE Travertine tiles frame a generous niche in a remodeled bathroom's wide-open stall shower.

LEFT A mix of compatible stone surfaces adds to the design distinction of this super-size luxury bath. A curved-front marble-topped vanity with two integral sinks coexists with a limestone floor and tub surround.

New York City's Empire State Building, erected in 1931, is a stellar example of the durability of limestone cladding in modern times. Limestone surfaces defy weather and temperature change, and successfully add texture and style to any exterior design. Houses clad entirely in limestone or travertine would

outdoor splash

be hard to find today, but those materials are often subtly included among the elements of exterior design. You can find them as trim around doors and windows; as quoins, columns, and keystones; and as steps, paths, and pool surrounds. Travertine, which is totally nonporous, makes an ideal patio surface. In every installation, these natural stone products add great character and style.

OPPOSITE TOP Austin White limestone forms the steps leading up to a Spanish-style Texas home. The same limestone also appears on retaining walls that support subtropical plantings flanking the stairway.

OPPOSITE BOTTOM Irregularly shaped blue-gray limestone was used to create the courtyard of this sprawling home. The entrance portion of the house is faced with locally quarried flagstone.

LEFT The architect of this stunning pavilion-style home chose limestone to surround a pool with a vanishing edge.

BELOW LEFT AND RIGHT The grandeur of this stone-surfaced outdoor dining room, shielded from the elements by a covered porch, is enhanced by a custom-designed honed-limestone table.

cool stones that warm the environment

I t takes millions of years to form, but slate—a fine-grained metamorphic rock—is created when mud, clay, volcanic ash, and stone sediment merge and harden after enduring enormous pressure and heat beneath the earth's surface. These evolving stresses cause the material to flatten and recrystallize, often at right angles to the direction of compression, typically called the bedding plane. That's what gives this rock its apparent grain, known in the stone world as "slate cleavage," which allows it to be split easily into thin sheets along one plane. Slate is a practical choice wherever it's used.

Slate Happens

| fireproof functionality |
| countertop variety | texture and tone |
| under foot |

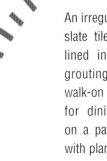

An irregular pattern of slate tiles, each out-lined in wide white grouting, forms a walk-on surface ideal for dining outdoors on a patio decorated with plants.

With its unique appearance, slate is rarely mistaken for other types of stone. Although lacking the sleekness of other stone forms, slate has intrinsic strength, density, and durability that make it equally usable on fireplaces, floors, walls, and countertops, providing a surface that needs little maintenance. Its versatility is supreme, which is why it is used so often on roofs, driveways, patios, pathways, and pool surrounds. Slate's most common colors are red, purple, tan, gray, green, and black. Like many natural stones, slate's rich coloration derives from its mineral content, which includes quartz, sericite, chlorite, and some graphite, plus mica, calcite, and trace quantities of numberless other minerals. The surface itself is not as hard as other stones, but it can be engraved easily.

fireproof functionality

ABOVE An old brick fireplace was given new life when covered with slate tiles cut to look like individual blocks of stone. Long strips of mahogany atop each level give the unit a finished look.

LEFT The stones that give this contemporary living room in a desert home the earthy richness its designer intended are Indian Rajah slate.

RIGHT Slate in tones called "Copper" and "West Country" create a striped effect for the towering fireplace that is the centerpiece of the living room in a house overlooking the San Francisco Bay. Set without visible grouting, the stones retain their striking individuality.

countertop variety

Although it is naturally water-resistant and requires sealing only after longtime heavy use, slate needs careful consideration when used as a work surface in a kitchen. It can create a rustic-looking surface of great beauty or one of smooth refinement, but in either case it can be easily chipped and scratched. Acid spills will not harm it, but in a kitchen—where a countertop receives daily use—a penetrating sealer is recommended. Choose one with a matte finish to ensure that the stone's natural color is unaltered.

ABOVE A slate countertop inset with a gas cooktop beneath wall-hung cupboards bridges two vertical cabinets, each with built-in appliances. This kitchen was remodeled to flow into the adjoining family room.

RIGHT Large slate tiles, each with its own color and pattern, surround an undermount sink in a master bath whose owners opted for an elegant country look.

BELOW Small slate tiles, each 4 in. sq., were installed to create a variegated look in a contemporary kitchen.

OPPOSITE Slate-wrapped and lit by under-cabinet halogens, this countertop in the corner of a kitchen in a nineteenth-century brownstone has plenty of room for individual activites.

ordering insights

▌ **Never finalize** a stone order based on looking at a single stone chip in a showroom; invest in three or four actual tiles to get a true picture of the color and pattern you prefer.

▌ **Then let the installer** add five to ten percent more stone than your blueprints suggest you need. There is always some waste when stone is cut and, occasionally, damage when the product is shipped.

▌ **When your order arrives,** inspect immediately to confirm its color and condition.

OPPOSITE In an open-plan kitchen that looks into the adjacent living room, jade-colored slate was used to fashion countertop surfaces plus a drop-in veined farm sink.

LEFT The shine of stainless-steel undermount sinks contrasts dramatically with the soft tone and texture of the surrounding honed-slate countertop.

BELOW Because slate is so easily cut with present-day machine tools, one end of this kitchen peninsula was shaped into an extended curve.

Added to its versatility and durability is slate's uniquely warm appearance, one that cannot be duplicated by any other type of stone. As a bonus, slate presents unrivaled earthi-

texture and tone

ness, and the colors apparent in individual slabs and tiles can vary widely, adding measurably to this stone's visual interest. Hand-splitting slate, when it is quarried, produces uneven sheets, so you may have to get used to its naturally cleft surface. Textural contrast results from pairing slate with glass, porcelain, and other more refined stone surfaces. True slate lovers tend to like the look.

LEFT Slate forms the base of an open step-down shower with rainshower head, and the dressing area that adjoins it in a beautifully comparmentalized master bath.

TOP Slate creates an earthy backsplash behind a porcelain tub. The trim strips have the same color as the 12 x 12-in. tiles but with a smoother finish.

ABOVE Two rows of 4-in.-sq. slate tiles, interrupted by a row of hand-set slate mosaics, create a finely detailed kitchen backsplash.

OPPOSITE A wall of beautifully colored Indian Rajah slate tiles works well with the Uba Tuba granite countertop in a lavish powder room.

Slate chips have long been used to make garden paths that drain well and are easy underfoot. But slate's indoor uses are becoming legendary, with installations that turn up not only in kitchens and baths—where water spills are frequent and undamaging—but

under foot

also in entry halls, living and dining rooms, family rooms designed for kick-back coziness, and stair treads and risers. That it's as much at home inside a house as outside—as garden walls, patio surface, and pool surrounds—points up its extreme versatility. Decorative products also come into play, as slate can be shaped into chairs, benches, lamp bases, and tabletops.

OPPOSITE Color, pattern, and textural contrasts are profoundly evident in this detail of a floor, which comprises slate tiles plus mosaic slate insets.

BELOW Tall translucent glass-block windows and a frameless glass-enclosed shower invite morning sun, flooding the pale slate floor of this peaches-and-cream-colored bath with light.

RIGHT The hearth is black granite; the fireplace wall is Italian plaster; and the floor of this contemporary living room is assembled from giant squares of Indian Rajah slate.

BELOW RIGHT White grouting underscores the geometry of the slate floor of this eat-in kitchen.

LEFT Like an earth-tone carpet, the tightly fit 12 x 12-in. slate tiles in this elegantly furnished dining room add subtle touches of texture to complete a serene setting.

BELOW Basque slate set in a checkerboard pattern provides functional balance in this stunning showcase kitchen. The curved panel on the sink front is wood finished to resemble burl.

RIGHT Ceramic tile and dark-stained wood partner with slate to create a dramatic mix of materials in this new master bath. Staggered rows of rectangular slate floor tiles add visual interest.

OPPOSITE A mix of natural stone varieties gives this sun-lit bathroom character and color. West Country slate gives individual floor tiles spark, and both black and copper-colored slate was striped on the tub surround, which ends at a frameless glass shower enclosure. The vanity countertop is granite.

▌

RIGHT An Indian Copper slate floor with autumnal tones adds a vibrant element to this expansive kitchen with an eat-in area set within a glass conservatory.

▌

BELOW Indian Rajah slate flooring ties the elements together in this open-plan home in the Southern California desert. Sand-colored walls and vaulted ceiling add lightness to an interior that is perennially sunny.

touch and feel

Slate's texture is determined by its physical composition, but the actual surface can be altered. For example, rough surfaces can be achieved from these techniques:

▌ **Split face:** a cut that produces an uneven surface.
▌ **Saw-cut:** a rough-sawn look complete with saw marks.
▌ **Flamed:** damp stone chipped off by an acetylene torch.
▌ **Sandblasted:** a pitted look determined by the grit used.

A smooth surface can be achieved by the following:

▌ **Honed:** smooth to the touch but does not show wear and tear.
▌ **Polished:** a mirror-like sheen that is best on walls and other surfaces that don't get abrasive contact.

LEFT Black slate grounds this comfortable family room, designed and furnished like a lavish outdoor patio.

BELOW Two wood finishes and two slate varieties dominate this L-shaped kitchen, where an island has a cantilevered counter corner.

OPPOSITE Wide at the bottom and narrow at the midpoint, this extraordinary set of stairs—treads as well as risers—is faced with slate. Stair extensions are where decorative items can be placed.

LEFT Irregularly shaped pieces of slate are knit together to create a patio outside a contemporary home. Recirculating pool water is pumped aboveground to create the waterfall.

ABOVE With a border of desert-style potted plants, oversize slate tiles in a mix of tones form a vast deck that extends outward, creating a platform for alfresco entertaining in a Southern California home.

BELOW Crudely cut but carefully shaped, a trio of slate slabs are stacked to form a step up to a columned front porch, a simple entrance to a stellar home.

spectacular variations

LEFT Pieces of slate were cut and pieced together to shape the coping around this elongated backyard pond.

BELOW LEFT Cottage-style wicker armchairs add traditional character to this slate dining patio.

BELOW A convenient shelter from untoward weather, a hip-roofed pavilion is the centerpiece of this pool-side patio, surfaced in squares of individually set slate tiles.

OPPOSITE Slate in a recurring pattern of stripes and squares pulls the eye outward, to the high brick fireplace at the end of this porch.

7

Soapstone, mined from quarries all over the world, is composed mostly of quartz along with talc and a variety of minerals that have been compressed and heated intensely for eons deep within the earth. Soapstone is actually a mineral called steatite that earned its common name because, when touched, it can feel like a piece of dry soap. Two types of soapstone are in use today. *Artistic* is relatively soft because of its ultra-high talc content, and is a favorite of artists because it can be carved so easily. *Architectural* is extremely dense, thus non-porous and virtually stain-resistant. It is also impervious to heat.

The Soapstone Story

❙ unique kitchen looks ❙
❙ wonder baths ❙ a colorful heritage ❙

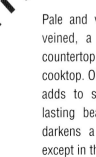

Pale and very lightly veined, a soapstone countertop envelops a cooktop. Oiling, which adds to soapstone's lasting beauty, often darkens a surface— except in this kitchen.

Because soapstone is water- and acid-resistant and is unfazed by temperature changes, it is a sensible choice for kitchen sinks as well as countertops. At the time it's pulled from the earth, it appears dark blue or gray but assumes other colors—light as well as dark—with age and constant use. Warm water mixed with kitchen detergent or any common household cleaner can be applied to clean a soapstone surface. It wears exceptionally well. In fact, the more it is used, the better it will look.

unique kitchen looks

ABOVE A brushed surface adds depth to soapstone's rich coloration, as shown in this detail of a Swedish wood-burning stove.

LEFT Unoiled soapstone can have a relatively light tone, as in this countertop in a kitchen with pale ceramic tile walls.

OPPOSITE TOP Dark gray, the color of most soapstones when mined, is enhanced by oiling, then polished to a sheen in this soapstone counter and farm sink.

OPPOSITE BOTTOM LEFT Elegantly shaped and cut, this soapstone countertop offers smoothness in contrast to the bead-board sides of wooden cabinetry.

OPPOSITE BOTTOM RIGHT Charcoal gray, another widely used color drawn from nature, frames this kitchen's farm sink surrounded by a soapstone counter and backsplash.

veining and variations

scratch free

As it's comparatively soft, soapstone may become nicked or dented over time. Such flaws give it a unique look and texture, but scratches are usually unwelcome.

- **For a light scratch,** apply a dab of mineral oil.
- **For deeper scratches,** rub 300 grit sandpaper or a sanding sponge on the afflicted area. The deeper the scratch, the more sanding is needed.
- **After sanding out the scratch,** apply a light coat of mineral oil to the area. Repeat the application two or three times during the next few days.

OPPOSITE TOP AND BOTTOM
A classic New England double sink is set into an unoiled countertop that extends around two sides of the kitchen in a contemporary log home. The soapstone was honed to create a matte finish, making the color less intense.

TOP LEFT With its chamfered edge, this one-piece sink and countertop has veining that gives depth to the soapstone's tone.

ABOVE AND LEFT Looking fresh and contemporary, this kitchen in the Chicago area has a polished soapstone counter with a grooved drainboard. Other elements rely on period designs: an unoiled soap-stone backsplash and farmhouse sink replicated from 100-year-old designs.

present and past

ecause it is rarer than other natural stones, soapstone is not as widely known or marketed. It is an exceptionally versatile product, however, useful in myriad applications such as benches, fireplaces, floors, stairways, and countertops. In bathrooms, its stone-by-stone variations are best seen in shower stalls and backsplashes that involve soapstone tiles rather than slabs, and its contrasts in color and veining create dramatic interest. When wet, soapstone has excellent traction, making bathroom floors particularly safe to walk on.

wonder baths

LEFT Charcoal gray with orange veining, these tiles in varied sizes include a shower, bench, and slip-free bathroom floor. The tub is set into a polished soapstone slab.

TOP A pair of hand-shaped vessel-style sinks carved out of the same soapstone as the tall backsplash sit on a pale slab of unoiled soapstone in an earthy bathroom setting.

ABOVE A luminous glass sink bowl is set on a square pedestal of unoiled soapstone, like the backsplash, and has tile supports.

ABOVE RIGHT A long bathroom sink and counter are assembled from strips and hung on the wall beneath a soapstone backsplash.

RIGHT Lengths of dark, oiled soapstone sur-round a sunken tub, but the walls above it are 12 x 12-in. soapstone tiles with white grout.

In colonial America, soapstone was quarried mainly in Vermont. Thus it can still be seen in vintage and historic homes throughout much of New England. Early Americans quickly recognized soapstone's amazing durability, shaping this product for use as fireplace hearths, sinks and all manner of work surfaces, plus the decorative fronts of the most elegant traditional wood stoves.

a colorful heritage

This is a stone that artisans appreciate because it carves so easily, using standard wood and masonry cutting tools. Although no two tiles or slabs are alike, soapstone can be installed so tightly that its seams never show. Most fabricators offer two primary finish choices: tumbled, which creates a slightly roughened surface, and honed, which tends to be much smoother.

ABOVE This custom-designed wood-burning stove is faced with soapstone cut to resemble ripples, like corrugated metal.

LEFT A shiny copper band defines the firebox opening in this gently curving fireplace. Soapstone tiles are arranged in stripes whose smoothness offsets the rough-textured stone wall.

OPPOSITE Soaring 10 ft. upward toward a vaulted ceiling, the pyramidal fireplace in this log home is a custom design that shows off both smooth and roughened soapstone dramatically.

mineral oil the miracle worker

Sandblasting enables artisans to engrave decorative images (right).

- **After soapstone is installed** and the adhesive has set, wipe off any accumulated dust and apply a coat of mineral oil.
- **Let this first coat sit** for a half hour before wiping away excess.
- **Repeat this process** once a week for six weeks. Then apply oil every other week, gradually stretching to once a month.
- **After a year,** you will need to re-oil only when the soapstone surface needs freshening.

8

Engineered stone is man-made, mostly of quartz, Earth's most abundant mineral. Manufacturing begins by blending quartz grains with pigments and polyester resin, then compressing to produce slabs that are cured, gauged to a precise thickness, and given a desired surface. These slabs may be cut into sheets for countertop or cladding applications. Engineered stone has no fissures, veins, or other flaws to compromise its quality. Installed, it often has a homogeneous appearance, which some people fault for having a less-than-natural look. This is no cheap imitation; its price is comparable to natural stone.

Engineered Hits

▎ lively colors ▎ great gains ▎
▎ a natural look outdoors ▎

Using manufactured stones arranged like random cobblestones, this custom outdoor fireplace is a durable addition to a covered porch decorated like a gracious living room.

E ngineered stone can be manufactured in many more colors than natural stone, thus offering more decorating flexibility. There is greater evenness in its patterning, and color matching is easy. If for example, there is a sudden need for additional kitchen counter surfaces, the exact same pattern, tone, and shade can be ordered and installed. Engineered stone is also more durable, as it is nonporous and both stain- and scratch-resistant. Any household cleanser can be used for routine maintenance, and no waxing or sealing is required. Some engineered products are formulated to resist mold, mildew, and bacteria.

lively colors

TOP A warm, even, brilliant tone pervades a kitchen counter whose curved profile is easy to achieve with the man-made product.

ABOVE A composite of concrete and recycled glass creates an unusual surface, giving a manufactured countertop its texture and tone.

RIGHT A soft peach tone—in the wood cabinets and in the honed countertop that surrounds the undermount sink— gives this kitchen uniform beauty.

OPPOSITE Slightly bowed, this breakfast counter was fabricated from engineered stone that complements the kitchen's ceramic tile walls.

OPPOSITE In this kitchen, the gleaming red engineered-stone counter and backsplash were used to set the color scheme for this "rose" treatment. The raised countertop surface beyond it is granite with an ogee edge.

TOP LEFT Engineered stone creates a smooth overall tone for this extended kitchen countertop.

TOP RIGHT An angled counter-top on two levels separates the dining area from the work zone without a divider to impede the overall flow of space.

MIDDLE The vast work surface of this kitchen is engineered stone, selected for its color as well as its durability.

BELOW This kitchen's dining bar, island, and main work counter are all topped with a soft-toned, lightly textured man-made stone.

IIIII dazzling consistent hues IIIIIIIIIIIIIIIIIIIIIIIIIIIIIIIIII

||||| natural depth and radiance |||||||||||||||||||||||||||||||||

OPPOSITE TOP LEFT In a brick-like installation, engineered stone on the staircase wall extends up to the ceiling.

OPPOSITE TOP RIGHT An even gray tone on a polished-stone surface creates a subtly reflective kitchen countertop.

OPPOSITE BOTTOM A speckled pattern creates a handsome look on this L-shaped counter.

ABOVE Stainless-steel accents are all that interrupts the subtle soft tones of this kitchen's walls, cabinets, and engineered-stone countertops.

LEFT In a kitchen with brushed-nickel fixtures and a stainless-steel sink, a glass-tile backsplash accents the polished quartz countertop.

In many ways, man-made stone is a miracle product, incomparable in its hardness and durability. It is also an amazing mimic. Some manufacturers have successfully created products that strongly resemble concrete, marble, travertine, and other natural stones—even granite. Unlike granite, however, there are no big swirls or color variations to give individual slabs and tiles strong visual contrast. Instead, there is great color uniformity; the color and natural mottling of quartz crystals occur throughout the product. Unlike any natural stone, sections can be replaced, if necessary, by product that matches the original exactly.

great gains

OPPOSITE Stretching from floor to ceiling, with a raised hearth and a notched-out space for collectibles, a man-made-stone fireplace and chimney breast are this living room's riveting focus.

ABOVE Framing a wide raised firebox is an installation of faux stones that are individually shaped to resemble hand-picked river rocks.

TOP RIGHT Wall panels fashioned from engineered stone add color and texture to an open-plan living-dining room. For this installation, individual stones were selected for their color and size, then placed to create a random look.

RIGHT Its stonelike treads, in a uniform color, add to the grandeur of a spiraling staircase in a Texas mansion. The tread product was chosen to withstand punishing use.

TOP LEFT AND LEFT Man-made stones applied to look like bricks add traditional touches to this newly built Southwestern-style home.

TOP RIGHT Stone veneer, installed in large sheets, creates a look that resembles the real thing in this textured house facade.

ABOVE AND OPPOSITE In a totally contemporary application, slabs of engineered stone in a brilliant orange tone were used as a decorative exterior wall panel and an outdoor fireplace surround.

OPPOSITE TOP Engineered stone adds texture and handmade elegance to the stuccoed exterior of a new English-style cottage with a flower-filled entry and steeply pitched roof system.

ngineered stone, in addition to its other notable properties, is immune to freezing and thawing problems and is burn resistant, although it could be damaged by prolonged exposure to high heat. (Trivets are recommended when transferring hot pots from cooktop to counter.) It is an ideal choice for exterior use because not even the fiercest elements of bad weather will alter its effectiveness. Stone walls are fashioned from large sheets of molded material that can be cut to fit whatever measurement is required. These sheets are relatively lightweight, thus easily installed, and the stones look convincingly natural.

a natural look outdoors

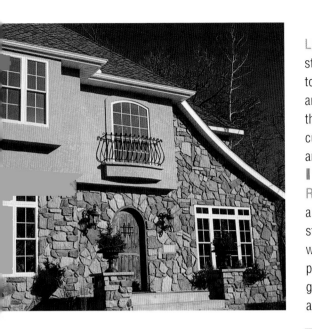

LEFT A mix of stucco and man-made stone lends character and interest to the exterior of a house with capstones and arches. All are fashioned from the same faux product that can be cut and shaped to fit any location and any architectural style.

RIGHT Man-made stone panels are used here as retaining walls, both straight and curved, and to cover the walls above the structural arches that provide views into a densely landscaped garden. The ledges and arch facing are also engineered stone.

RIGHT What seems to be a clapboard wall is actually engineered stone, selected not only for its appearance but also for its long-wearing capacity. The "individual strips" of siding are actually panels of molded material, cut to fit the house's exterior elevation.

BELOW "Fallingwater" by the architect Frank Lloyd Wright inspired this home's design. It uses stucco and engineered stone to evoke Wright's houses with a horizontal thrust and mixed materials.

Resource Guide

Accent Marble Company, Inc.
www.accentmarble.com
800-880-1103
Manufactures cultured marble, cultured granite, and acrylic products.

Alexander Baer Associates Incorporated
410-727-4100
Interior designer

Atsushi Tomioka
www.tomiinterior.com
212-941-5878
Photographer

Anne Gummerson
www.annegummersonphoto.com
Photographer

Annie Gevorkian
Designer Touch LLC
702-304-0212
Interior designer

Art & Maison
www.artandmaison.com
305-948-0477
Creates custom concrete sinks, tubs, countertops, and mosaics.

Becker Architectural Concrete
www.beckerconcrete.com
651-554-0346
Designs and constructs architectural-concrete products.

Benning Design Associates
www.benningdesign.com
916-448-8120
Interior Designer

Beryn Hammil Designs
www.BHammil.com
415-924-5509
Interior designer

Beth Singer
www.bethsingerphotographer.com
Photographer

Bob Lefferts Photography
boblefferts1@aol.com
Photographer

Bomanite Corporation
www.bomanite.com
559-673-2411
Manufactures decorative concrete products.

Boulder Creek
www.bouldercreekstone.com
763-786-7138
Manufactures stone veneer, thin brick, tile pavers, and accessories.

Brennan+Company Architects
www.brennanarch.com
410-788-2289
Architect

Brian Swanson
SWANSON Design
www.swanson-design.com
410-377-2750
Architect and interior designer

Brookhaven Cabinets
www.wood-mode.com
877-635-7500
Manufactures custom cabinetry.

Brukoff Design Associates, Inc.
www.brukoffdesign.com
415-332-6350
Interior designer

Buddy Rhodes Studio
www.buddyrhodes.com
877-706-5303
Manufactures decorative concrete products.

Cambria
www.cambriaUSA.com
866-226-2742
Manufactures natural quartz surfaces.

Cameron Carothers Photography
www.carothersphoto.com
Photographer

The following list of manufacturers, designers, and photographers is meant to be a general guide to industry and product-related sources represented by the photographs in this book.

Carolyn Bates
carolyn.bates7@verizon.net
Photographer

Catherine Clemens, ASLA
Clemens & Associates, Inc.
505-982-4005
Landscape architect

Cheng Design
www.chengdesign.com
510-849-3272
Interior design and manufacturers of kitchen and bath products.

Chesney's Inc.
www.chesneys-usa.com
404-948-1111
Supplier of antique and reproduction stone mantels.

Chris McBrayer
www.fivept.com
804-307-7709
Manufactures decorative concrete products.

Chris Lewis Architects
www.chrislewisarchitects.com
512-474-8124
Architect

Countercast Designs, Inc
888-787-2278
www.countercast.com
Produces precast concrete countertops and sinks.

Cuellar Cosentino USA
www.cuellarusa.com
800-291-1311
Manufactures architectural stone products.

Cultured Stone
Owens Corning
www.culturedstone.com
800-255-1727
Manufactures stone veneer.

Dave Adams
www.daveadamsphotography.com
Photographer

David Anderson
www. daphoto.com
Photographer

David Duncan Livingston
www.davidduncanlivingston.com
Photographer

Daryl Savage
DHS Design
www.dhsdesigns.com
410-827-8167
Importer of antiques and antiquities.

Decolav
www.decolav.com
561-274-2110
Manufactures plumbing products.

Donald Schnell
www.donaldschnell.com
800-253-7107
Creates handcrafted ceramics.

Dorado Soapstone
303-412-1093
www.doradosoapstone.com
Supplier of natural Brazilian soapstone.

Resource Guide

Echeguren Slate
www.echeguren.com
415-206-9343
Importer, exporter, and distributor of slate flooring.

Eldorado Stone
www.eldoradostone.com
800-925-1491
Manufactures architectural stone veneer.

Elizabeth Spengler
Dorado Designs
www.doradodesigns.com
866-577-1800
Interior designer specializing in kitchens and baths.

Elsa Kessler
Quintessentials
212-877-1919
Interior designer

Emily Castle, ASID
Castle Design
www.emilycastle.com
314-591-8651
Interior designer

Erwin & Sons Direct Imports, Inc.
770-579-0414
Manufactures residential rattan and wicker.

EVERETT & SOULE
Architectural Photographers
www.portfolios.com/everettandsoule
407-831-4183
Photographer

FORMA Design, Inc.
Andreas Charalambous, AIA, IIDA
www.FORMAonline.com
Architect and interior designer

Formica
www.formica.com
800-FORMICA
Manufactures surfaces.

Gabrielle Kessler for folio.photography
gabriellekessler@hotmail.com
Photographer

Geoff Hodgdon
www.geoffreyhodgdon.com
202-246-2058
Photographer

George Snead
207-882-4185
Interior designer

Granite Solutions
Benissimo Systems
www.benissimosystems.com
Manufactures surfaces.

Granite Transformations
northjersey@granitetransformations.com
201-933-8500
Manufactures granite surfaces.

Green and Company
www.GreenandCompanyDesign.com
212-906-0110
Interior design, decorating, and arcitectural firm.

Green Mountain Soapstone Corporation
www.greenmountainsoapstone.com
802-468-5636
Manufactures soapstone countertops.

Green River Stone Company
www.greenriverstone.com
800-443-1607
Supplies fossil fish murals and stone products.

Hart Stoneworks
www.soapstoneofcolorado.com
866-344-7484
Manufactures soapstone sinks, countertops and tile.

Hy-Lite Products, Inc.
www.hy-lite.com
800-827-3691
Manufactures acrylic-block products.

Icestone
www.icestone.biz
718-624-4900
Manufactures surfaces made of recycled glass and concrete.

Ivy D
imoriber@optonline.net
Photographer

James Hardie Building Products
www.jameshardie.com
888 J-HARDIE
Manufactures fiber cement siding, backerboard, and pipe.

Janice Stone Thomas, ASID, CKD
StoneWood Design, Inc.
www.stonewooddesign.com
916-454-1506
Interior designer

Jeanine Veldhuis
Veldhuis Interior Design
949-723-9330
Interior designer

Joan DesCombes, CKD
Architectural Artworks, Inc.
www.arch-art.com
407-644-1410
Designs interior architecture and custom cabinetry.

John A. Buscarello, Inc.
www.buscarello.com
212-691-5881
Interior designer

Keith Mazzei
DiSalvo Interiors
www.disalvointeriors.com

516-873-6011
Interior designer

Ken Burghardt
Studio Mehler
www.studiomehler.com
415-864-0800
Manufactures custom cabinetry.

Kohler Company
www.kohler.com
800-456-4537
Manufacturers plumbing products.

Lou Ann Bauer, ASID
Bauer Design
www.bauerdesign.com
415-282-2788
Interior designer

Maureen Consolé Interiors
631-757-0002

Madrone Custom Cabinetry
www.madronecustomcabinetry.com
866-914-9663
Manufactures custom cabinetry.

Mark Cutler Designs
www.markcutlerdesign.com
310-360-6212
Interior designer

Mark Samu
www.samustudios.com
Photographer

melabee m miller
mmiller95@aol.com
Photographer

Michael Merrill ASID
Michael Merrill Design Studio
www.michaelmerrill.net
415-440-2111
Interior designer

Michael Milne
Barefoot Architect, Inc

Resource Guide

www.barefootaia.com
Interior designer

Miro Rivera Architects
www.mirorivera.com
412-477-7016
Architect

Neumann Smith and Associates
www.neumannsmith.com
248-352-8310
Architect and interior designer

Nic Holland Architect Inc.
512-422-5621
Architect

Oso Industries
www.osoindustries.com
347-365-0389
Design studio focusing on decorative concrete.

Pat Stockton, CID
www.indesign-patstockdon.com
804-272-9504
Interior designer

Paul Bardagjy
www.bardagjyphoto.com
Photographer

Peter Tata Photography
ptata@austin.rr.com
Photographer

Phllip Clayton Thompson
pizzithompson@comcast.net
Photographer

Pyrolave USA
www.pyrolave.com
919-788-8953
Manufactures enameled lava products.

Quintessentials
212-877-1919
Interior designer

Rachel Lerner
Legend Homes
www.legendhomes.com
503-620-8080
Homebuilder

Rick Rogers, ASID
916-213-3697
Interior designer

RMG Stone Products
www.rmgstone.com
802-468-5636
Manufactures marble and granite products.

Rob Melnychuk
www.robmelnychuk.com
Photographer

Sally Power Interiors
www.powerinteriors.com
415-621-9991
Interior designer

Sergio Fama
www.sergiofama.com
Photographer

Shasta Smith, Allied ASID
www.shastasmith.com
916-871-2892
Interior designer

Silestone
www.silestoneusa.com
800-291-1311
Manufactures quartz surfaces.

Sisler Builders
www.sislerbuilders.com
802-244-5672
Homebuilder

Soft As Stone
www.softasstone.com
218-834-7800
Manufactures decorative concrete products.

Sonoma Cast Stone
www.sonomastone.com
877-283-2400
Manufactures decorative concrete products.

Stone Forest
www.stoneforest.com
888-682-2987
Manufactures decorative granite products.

Stoneyard
www.stoneyard.com
800-231-2200
Manufactures stone products.

StoneAge Designs
www.stoneagedesigns.net
404-350-3333
Manufactures stone products.

Stuart Ortel
www.stonehilldesignassociates.com
410-464-2000
Landscape architects

Todd Caverly
www.toddcaverly.com
Photographer

Tria Giovan
triag@earthlink.net
Photographer

Tulikivi Corporation

www.tulikivi.com
Manufactures soapstone products.

Vasi Ypsilantis, CKD
www.thebreakfastroom.com
516-365-7713
Interior designer specializing in kitchens.

Whitecraft, Inc.
www.whitecraft.net
800-790-8677
Makes handcrafted furniture.

Widstrand Photography
www.widstrand.com
Photographer

Thomas Lipps
tlipps@ormondbeach.org
386-676-3224
Photographer

Timberlake Cabinet Company
www.timberlake.com
Manufactures cabinetry.

ULRICH INC.
www.ulrichkitchen.com
201-445-1260
Designs and builds kitchens.

Walter David Brown Architects
www.walterdavidbrown.com
212-431-3779
Architect and interior designer

Glossary

Actual Dimensions: The measured dimensions of a masonry unit as opposed to its nominal size that includes mortar joints.

Aggregate: Crushed stone, gravel, or other material added to cement to make concrete or mortar. Gravel and crushed stone are considered coarse aggregate; sand is considered fine aggregate.

Concave Joint: A masonry joint that is recessed and formed in mortar. A curved steel jointing tool is used to make a concave joint.

Concrete: A mixture of portland cement, sand, gravel or crushed rock, and water that forms a solid material when cured.

Concrete Block: A masonry unit that consists of an out-side shell with a hollow center that is divided by two or three vertical webs.

Concrete Pavers: Commonly used for driveways, patios, and sidewalks; available in many shapes and sizes.

Control Joints: Surface joints that allow concrete stress cracks to form in straight lines at planned locations.

Curing: Providing proper moisture, typically to a concrete slab, so that the miz reaches maximum strength without cracking or shrinking.

Cut Stone: Any stone that has been milled or worked by hand to a specific shape or dimensions.

Darby: A long-handled tool used for smoothing the surface of a concrete slab.

Dressed Stone: Usually quarried stone that has been squared-off on all sides and has a smooth face.

Edging Joints: The rounded-over edges of a pour that are resistant to cracking and chipping.

Face: The exposed side of a stone.

Fieldstone: Stone as it is found in the natural environment.

Flagstone: Any stone milled to a uniform thickness of 1 to 2 inches to use for walk and patio surfaces. Flagstone is available in uniform rectangular shapes or in random shaped pieces sometimes called crazy paving.

Flagstone Patterning: Carving a design onto the surface of concrete to make a pattern.

Flashing: Masonry flashing can be made of metal, rubberized asphalt sheet membranes, or other materials. It controls moisture in masonry walls by keeping the top of a wall dry.

Floating: The process of smoothing the surface of a concrete pour with a float made of steel, aluminum, magnesium, or wood. This action raises fine particles and water to the surface.

Footing: Support for mortared stonework generally made of concrete and extending below the frost line to avoid problems from frost heaves.

Formwork: The forms, often staked and braced two-by lumber, that contain wet concrete.

Mortar: A mixture of cementitious materials, fine aggregate, and water. Mortar is used to bond bricks or blocks.

Normal Dimensions: The measured dimensions of a masonry unit plus one mortar joint; generally rounding up the actual fractional dimension of the unit.

Pavers: Any stone milled to a uniform size and shape, typically about the size of a brick, and used to surface walkways and patios.

Prepackaged Concrete Mix: A mix that combines cement, sand, and gravel in the correct proportions and requires only the addition of water to create fresh concrete.

Quarry Dressed: Stone that is squared-off on all sides but has a rough face. Sometimes called semi-dressed stone.

Ready-Mix Concrete: Wet concrete that is transported from a concrete supplier. The concrete is ready to pour.

Rebar: Reinforcing bar that is used for concrete that will carry a heavy load, such as footings, foundation walls, columns, and pilasters.

Reinforcing Mesh: Steel wires woven or welded into a grid of 6- or 10-inch squares. The mesh is used primarily to reinforce concrete in flatwork, such as sidewalks, patios, and driveways.

Screeding: Moving a straight board, such as a 2x4, back and forth across the tops of forms to smooth and level sand or concrete.

Segregation: A condition that results when concrete is overworked—such as when trying to remove air bubbles—and the mix components separate.

Steel Reinforcement: Reinforcing mesh or rebar that is used to strengthen concrete and masonry walls; generally placed horizontally (in pairs) in concrete footings and vertically to reinforce block foundation walls.

Tamp: Compacting gravel or sand in 2- to 4-inch layers to form a solid base for flat stonework, such as a patio.

Tamper: A hand tool or power device used to compact soil or gravel so that it is less likely to shift or crumble.

Troweling: Finishing the concrete after it has been screeded. This finishing step is mainly for interior concrete without air-entrainment.

Index

Photo Credits

T: Top R: Right B: Bottom L: Left C: Center

page 1: design: Lou Ann Bauer, ASID, Bauer Design **page 4:** photo: Peter Tata **page 5:** photo: Gabrielle Kessler, courtesy Brookhaven Cabinets, a division of Wood-Mode, design: Elsa Kessler, Quintessentials **page 6:** (T) photo: Peter Tata; (C) photo and design: Brukoff Design Associates, Inc.; (B) courtesy of Chesney's Inc. **page 7:** photo and design: Brukoff Design Associates, Inc. **pages 8–9:** photo: www.davidduncanlivingston.com, design: Benning Design Associates **page 10:** (T) courtesy of Sonoma Cast Stone; (C) courtesy of Countercast Designs, Inc.; (B) design: Becker Architectural Concrete **page 11:** courtesy of Chesney's Inc., The Jasper Conran Collection **page 12:** (T) photo: Phillip Clayton-Thompson, styling: Donna Pizzi; (B) courtesy of Soft As Stone **page 13:** photo: Widstrand Photography **page 14:** courtesy of Sonoma Cast Stone **page 15:** photo: Tony Giammarino/Giammarino & Dworkin, design: Pat Stockdon, CID, concrete design: Chris McBrayer **page 16:** (T) design: Andreas Charalambous, AIA, IIDA, FORMA Design; photo: Goeff Hodgdon; (B) photo: Sergio Fama, courtesy of Art & Maison, Inc. **page 17:** (T) design: Andreas Charalambous, AIA, IIDA, FORMA Design; photo: Goeff Hodgdon; (B) courtesy of Art & Maison, Inc. photo: Sergio Fama **page 18:** (T) photo: Peter Tata Photography, architect: Chris Lewis Architects; (B) photo: Sergio Fama, courtesy of Art & Maison, Inc. **page 19:** photo: Tria Giovan **page 20:** courtesy of Bomanite Corporation, North Texas Bomanite, Dallas **page 21:** (TL, C) courtesy of Bomanite, Wm. Aupperle & Sons Construction, Morton, IL; (TR) design: Becker Architectural Concrete **page 22:** photo: Goeff Hodgdon, design: Andreas Charalambous, AIA, IIDA, FORMA Design **page 23:** (TL) courtesy of Soft As Stone; (TR) courtesy of Countercast Designs, Inc.; (C) photo: Sergio Fama, courtesy of Art & Maison, Inc.; (B) courtesy of Countercast Designs, Inc.

page 24–25: (TL) photo: Paul Bardagjy; (B, R) photo: Sergio Fama, courtesy of Art & Maison, Inc. **page 26:** (T, BR) photo: Sergio Fama, courtesy of Art & Maison, Inc.; (BL) photo: Tria Giovan **page 27:** (T) photo: Sergio Fama, courtesy of Art & Maison, Inc.; (B) photo: Tony Giammarino/Giammarino & Dworkin, cabinetry: Madrone Custom Cabinetry **page 28:** (T) photo: Goeff Hodgdon, design: Andreas Charalambous, AIA, IIDA, FORMA Design; (BL) photo: Sergio Fama, courtesy of Art & Maison, Inc.; (BR) courtesy of Sonoma Cast Stone **page 29:** photo: Sergio Fama, courtesy of Art & Maison, Inc. **page 30:** photo: Beth Singer **page 31:** (TL, TR) photo: Sergio Fama, courtesy of Art & Maison, Inc.; (BR) photo: Beth Singer **page 32:** (T) design: Andreas Charalambous, AIA, IIDA, FORMA Design; photo: Goeff Hodgdon; (B) photo: Sergio Fama, courtesy of Art & Maison, Inc. **page 33:** (TL) photo: Sergio Fama, courtesy of Art & Maison, Inc.; (TR) courtesy of Countercast Designs, Inc.; (B) photo: Goeff Hodgdon, design: Andreas Charalambous, AIA, IIDA, FORMA Design **page 34–35:** design: Lou Ann Bauer, ASID, Bauer Design **page 36:** photo: Sergio Fama, courtesy of Art & Maison, Inc. **page 37:** (TL) design: Lou Ann Bauer, ASID, Bauer Design; (TR) photo: Sergio Fama, courtesy of Art & Maison, Inc.; (B) courtesy of Timberlake Cabinet Company **page 38–39:** design: Lou Ann Bauer, ASID, Bauer Design **page 40:** (T) design: Becker Architectural Concrete; (B) courtesy of Soft As Stone, design: Ulrich, Inc. **page 41:** (T) courtesy of Sonoma Cast Stone; (B) photo: Sergio Fama, courtesy of Art & Maison, Inc. **page 42:** (TR, BL) courtesy of Sonoma Cast Stone; (BR) design: Lou Ann Bauer, ASID, Bauer Design **page 43:** design: Cheng Design **page 44:** photo: Tria Giovan **page 45:** (TL, B) design: Lou Ann Bauer, ASID, Bauer Design; (LC) courtesy of Countercast Designs, Inc.; (CR) courtesy of Soft As Stone **page 46:** (TR) courtesy Soft As Stone; (C) courtesy of

Countercast Designs, Inc.; (B) design: Becker Architectural Concrete **page 47:** (T) design: Cheng Design; (B) photo: Sergio Fama, courtesy of Art & Maison, Inc. **page 48–49:** courtesy of Bomanite Corporation, Progressive Concrete Works, Phoenix, AZ **page 50:** photo: Tria Giovan **page 51:** (T) design: Green and Company; (C) courtesy of Bomanite Corporation **page 52:** (T) courtesy of Bomanite Corporation; (B) design: Becker Architectural Concrete **page 53:** photo: Robert Melnychuk **page 54:** (TR) photo: Anne Gummerson Photography, design: DHS Design; (CL) design: Buddy Rhodes, Buddy Rhodes Concrete Products; (B) photo: Tria Giovan **page 55:** photo: Anne Gummerson Photography, design: DHS Design **page 56:** courtesy of OSO Industries **page 57:** photo: Anne Gummerson Photography, design: DHS Design **page 58–59:** photo: Todd Caverly, design: George Snead, Jr. **page 60:** photo: Rob Melnychuk **page 61:** (T) photo: Tria Giovan; (B) photo: Anne Gummerson Photography **page 62:** (L) photo: Anne Gummerson Photography; (R) courtesy of www.stoneyard.com; (B) courtesy of Erwin & Sons **page 63:** (L) photo: Rob Melnychuk; (CR) courtesy of Pyrolave USA **page 64:** photo: Paul Bardijy **page 65:** (TL) Paul Bardijy; (TR) photo:

Cameron Carothers Photography, design: Jeanine Veldhuis, Veldhuis Interior Design; (B) photo: Rob Melnychuk **page 66:** (TL) courtesy of StoneAge Designs, design: Scagliola Stone Collection by Thierry Francois; (TR, B) photos: Anne Gummerson Photography **page 67:** photo: Anne Gummerson Photography **page 68:** (BL) photo: Anne Gummerson Photography; (C) courtesy of www.stoneyard.com; (TR) photo: Rob Melnychuk **page 69:** photo: Ivy Moriber Neal/Ivy D Photography, Inc., design: Maureen Console, M. Console Interiors **page 70:** photo: Anne Gummerson Photography, design: Stuart Ortel, Stone Hill Design **page 71:** (T) photo: Ivy Moriber Neal/Ivy D Photography, Inc., design: Maureen Console, M. Console Interiors; (B) courtesy of www.stoneyard.com **page 72:** (TL) photo: Anne Gummerson Photography; (CL, CR) courtesy of www.stoneyard.com; (B) photo: Carolyn L. Bates, landscape architect: Catherine Clemens, Clemens & Associates, Inc. **page 73:** photo: Carolyn L. Bates, landscape architect: Catherine Clemens, Clemens & Associates, Inc., design: Thomas Lipps **page 74:** (T) photo: EVERETT & SOULE, design: Joan DesCombes, CKD, Architectural Artworks; (L) photo: Anne Gummerson Photography **page 75:** courtesy of Stone Age Designs, design: Scagliola Stone Collection by Thierry Francois **page 76:** (TL, B) design: Janice Stone Thomas, ASID, CKD; (TR) photo: Tria Giovan **page 77:** (T) design: Stone Age Designs, Scagliola Stone Collection by Thierry Francois; (L) courtesy of Pyrolave USA **page 78:** (T, B) courtesy of Stone Forest **page 79:** design: Benning Design Associates **page 80:** (T) courtesy of Stone Forest; (B) courtesy of Cuellar Cosentino USA **page 81:** (TL, C, TR) courtesy of Stone Forest **page 82:** (TL) courtesy of Hy-Lite; (TR) courtesy of Stone Forest; (B) courtesy of Cuellar Cosentino USA **page 83:** (L) photo: Bob Lefferts Photography, design: Donald Schnell, Artistic Villas; (TR, B) courtesy of Cuellar

Cosentino USA **page 84:** (TL, TR) courtesy of Stone Forest; (B) photo: Cameron Carothers Photography, design: Mark Cutler, Mark Cutler Design, Inc. **page 85:** (TL, TR) courtesy of Stone Forest; (B) photo: www.davidduncanlivingston.com, design: Benning Design Associates **page 86:** (T) photo: Rob Melnychuk; (B) photo: Beth Singer **page 87:** photo: Rob Melnychuk **page 88:** photo: (TL) melabee m miller; (TR) photo: Beth Singer; (B) photo: Rob Melnychuk **page 89:** photo: melabee m miller **page 90:** (T) photo: Beth Singer; (B) photo: Mark Samu **page 91:** photo: Todd Caverly **page 92:** (T) photo: Todd Caverly; (B) photo: Rob Melnychuk **page 93:** courtesy of Green River

Stone **page 94:** (TR) photo: Tria Giovan; (C, B) courtesy of Stone Forest **page 95:** (Both) courtesy of Stone Forest **page 96:** photo: Anne Gummerson **page 97:** photo: David Anderson **page 98:** (TR, BR) courtesy of Granite Transformations; (BL) photo: Carolyn Bates, design: Steve Sisler **page 99:** photo: David Anderson, architect: Walter Brown **page 100:** (TL) courtesy Granite Transformations; (BL, R) photo: Gabrielle Kessler, courtesy of Quintessentials, design: Elsa Kessler, cabinets: Brookhaven "Vista" **page 101:** photo: Gabrielle Kessler, courtesy of Quintessentials, design: Elsa Kessler, cabinetry: Brookhaven "Vista" **page 102:** photo: EVERETT & SOULE, design: Joan

Photo Credits

DesCombes, CKD, Architectural Artworks Incorporated **page 103:** (TL, BR) photos: EVERETT & SOULE, design: Joan DesCombes, CKD, Architectural Artworks Incorporated; (TR) courtesy of Granite Transformations **page 104–105:** (All) photos: EVERETT & SOULE, design: Joan DesCombes, CKD, Architectural Artworks Incorporated **page 106:** photo: Todd Caverly **page 107:** (TL, BR) photos: Dave Adams, design: Shasta Smith, Allied ASID, Delicate Design; (TR) design: John Buscarello, ASID (BL) photo: Todd Caverly **page 108:** (T) design: Emily Castle, ASID, Castle Design; (B) courtesy of Granite Transformations **page 109:** photo: EVERETT & SOULE, design: Joan DesCombes, CKD, Architectural Artworks Incorporated **page 110:** courtesy of Stone Forest **page 111:** (T) courtesy of Stone Forest; (B) courtesy of Granite Transformations **page 112:** (TL, C) design: Rick Rogers, ASID; (TR) photo and design: Beryn Hammil; (B) courtesy of Granite Transformations **page 113:** photo and design: Beryn Hammil **page 114:** design:

Emily Castle, ASID, Castle Design **page 115:** (R) photo: EVERETT & SOULE, design: Joan DesCombes, CKD, Architectural Artworks Incorporated; (B) courtesy of Granite Transformations **page 116–117:** photo: Bob Lefferts Photography, design: Michael Milne and Helen Simon **page 118:** (T) courtesy of Chesney's Inc.; (B) photo: Beth Singer **page 119–123:** courtesy of Chesney's Inc. **page 124:** design: Janice Stone Thomas, ASID, CKD **page 125:** (T) photo: Anne Gummerson Photography; (BL) design: Janice Stone Thomas, ASID, CKD; (BR) photo: Anne Gummerson Photography, design: Darryl Savage **page 126:** (T) photo: Bob Lefferts Photography; (B) courtesy of Kohler **page 127:** photo: Anne Gummerson Photography, architect: Brian Swanson **page 128:** photo: EVERETT & SOULE, design: Joan DesCombes, CKD, Architectural Artworks Incorporated **page 129:** (T) courtesy of Decolav; (B) photo: Bob Lefferts Photography **page 130:** (T) courtesy of Stone Forest; (BL) photo: melabee m miller; (BR) design: Michael Merrill Design Studio **page 131:**

photo: Beth Singer, architect: Neumann & Smith Associates, design: Andrea Sachse **page 132:** (T) photo: Anne Gummerson Photography, design: Alexander Baer; (B) photo: EVERETT & SOULE, design: Joan DesCombes, CKD, Architectural Artworks Incorporated **page 133:** (T) photo: Anne Gummerson Photography; (BL) photo: Beth Singer; (BR) photo: www.davidduncanlivingston.com, design: Sally Power Interiors **page 134–135:** photo and design: Brukoff Design Associates, Inc. **page 136:** (T) photo and design: Brukoff Design Associates, Inc.; (B) design: John A. Buscarello, ASID **page 137:** photo: Cameron Carothers Photography, design: Rachel Lerner for Legend Homes **page 138:** courtesy of Chesney's **page 139:** (TL, TR) courtesy of Chesney's; (C) photo and design: Brukoff Design Associates, Inc. **page 140:** (T) courtesy of Brookhaven Cabinets, a division of Wood-Mode, design: Elizabeth Spengler, Dorado Designs; (B) photo and design: Brukoff Design Associates, Inc. **page 141:** courtesy of Brookhaven Cabinets, a division of Wood-Mode, design: Elizabeth Spengler, Dorado Designs **page 142:** photo and design: Brukoff Design Associates, Inc. **page 143:** (T) design: Janice Stone Thomas, ASID, CKD; (B) design: John A. Buscarello, ASID; photo: Atsushi Tomioka **page 144:** photo: Paul Bardagjy, architect: Nik Holland **page 145:** (T) design: Janice Stone Thomas, ASID, CKD; (C) design: Michael Merrill Design Studio; (BL) photo and design: Brukoff Design Associates, Inc. **page 146:** (T, B) photos: Peter Tata **page 147:** (T) photo: Paul Bardagjy, architect: Miro Rivera Architects; (BL, BR) design: Michael Merrill Design Studio **page 148–149:** photo: Anne Gummerson Photography **page 150:** (T) photo: Anne Gummerson Photography, architect: Brennan + Company Architects; (B) photo and design: Brukoff Design Associates **page 151:** photo and design: Brukoff Design Associates **page 152:** (T) photo: Gabrielle Kessler, courtesy Brookhaven Cabinets, a

division of Wood-Mode, design: Elsa Kessler, Quintessentials; (C) design: Janice Stone Thomas, CKD, ASID; (B) photo: Mark Samu **page 153:** photo: Gabrielle Kessler, courtesy Brookhaven Cabinets, a division of Wood-Mode, design: Elsa Kessler, Quintessentials **page 154–155:** photos: courtesy DIY Network's Kitchen Renovations series and RMG Stone Products **page 156:** (T) photo: Cameron Carothers Photography; (CR) courtesy of Echeguren Slate, design: Ken Burghardt, Studio Mehler; (B) photo: Paul Bardagjy **page 157:** photo and design: Brukoff Design Associates **page 158:** (T) design: Ken Burghardt, Studio Mehler; (B) photo: Dave Adams, design: Shasta Smith, Allied ASID **page 159:** (T) photo and design: Brukoff Design Associates; (B) photo: melabee m miller **page 160:** (T) photo and design: Brukoff Design Associates; (B) photo: Ivy D Photography Inc., design: Vasi Ypsilantis, The Breakfast Room, Ltd. **page 161:** photo: Anne Gummerson Photography, architect: Brennan + Company Architects **page 162–163:** photos and design: Brukoff Design Associates **page 164:** (T) photo: Rob Melychuk; (B) photo and design: Brukoff Design Associates **page 165:** courtesy of Echeguren Slate, photo and design: Brukoff Design Associates **page 166:** photo: Paul Bardajy **page 167:** (T) photo and design: Brukoff Design Associates; (B) photo: Carolyn L. Bates **page 168:** (T) photo: Anne Gummerson Photography; (BL) courtesy of Whitecraft, Inc.; (BR) photo: Ivy D Photography Inc., design: Keith Mazzei, DiSalvo Interiors **page 169:** photo: Tria Giovan **page 170–171:** courtesy of Sensa by Cosentino **page 172:** (T) courtesy of Tulikivi; (B) courtesy of Hart Stoneworks and Green Mountain Soapstone **page 173:** (T, BL) courtesy of Hart Stoneworks and Green Mountain Soapstone; (BR) courtesy of Green Mountain Soapstone **page 174:** courtesy of Green Mountain Soapstone **page 175:** (TL) courtesy of

Sensa by Cosentino; (TR, B) courtesy of Hart Stoneworks and Green Mountain Soapstone; **page 176:** courtesy of Hart Stoneworks and Green Mountain Soapstone **page 177:** (T, CL, CR) courtesy of Dorado Soapstone; (BR) courtesy of Green Mountain Soapstone **page 178–179:** courtesy of Tulikivi **page 180–181:** courtesy of Eldorado Stone **page 182:** design: John A. Buscarello ASID **page 183:** (T, B)courtesy of Silestone; (C) courtesy of Icestone **page 184:** photo: EVERETT & SOULE, design: Joan DesCombes, CKD, Architectural Artworks Incorporated **page 185:** (TL) courtesy of Formica; (TR, C, B) courtesy of Cambria **page 186:** (TL) courtesy of Eldorado Stone; (TR, B) courtesy of Formica **page 187:** (T) courtesy of Cambria; (B) photo: Mark Samu **page 188:** courtesy of Boulder Creek **page 189:** (T, C) courtesy of Boulder Creek; (B) courtesy of Cambria **page 190:** (TL, B) courtesy of Eldorado

Stone; (TR) courtesy of Boulder Creek; (C) courtesy of Pyrolave USA **page 191:** (T) courtesy of Cultured Stone; (B) courtesy of Pyrolave USA **page 192:** (T) courtesy of Boulder Creek; (C) courtesy of James Hardie Building Products, Inc.; (B) design: Annie Gevorkian, ASID, Designer Touch **page 193:** courtesy of Cultured Stone **page 195:** photo: EVERETT & SOULE, design: Joan DesCombes, CKD, Architectural Artworks Incorporated **page 196:** courtesy of Stone Forest **page 199:** courtesy of Accent Marble **page 204:** courtesy of Benning Design Associates **page 205:** courtesy of Brookhaven Cabinets **page 206:** courtesy of Designer Touch **page 207:** photo: Anne Gummerson Photography

If you like
Design Ideas for Decorative Concrete & Stone,
take a look at the rest of the
Design Idea series

Design Ideas for Kitchens provides design inspiration for creating an attractive, up-to-date kitchen. Contains hundreds of photographs and a wealth of information. *Paper with flaps.*

Over 500 photographs.
224 pp.
$ 19.95 (US)
$ 24.95 (CAN)
BOOK #: 279415

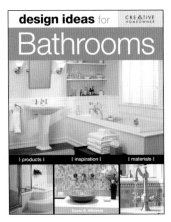

Design Ideas for Bathrooms offers hundreds of color photographs and extensive information on the latest trends in design, materials, and related products. *Paper with flaps.*

Over 500 photographs.
224 pp.
$ 19.95 (US)
$ 24.95 (CAN)
BOOK #: 279268

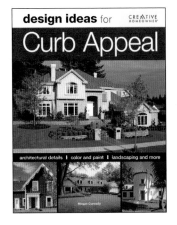

Design Ideas for Curb Appeal shows how to make the outside of the home look its very best. Entryways, windows, siding, landscaping, and more are covered. *Paper with flaps.*

Over 300 photographs.
208 pp.
$ 19.95 (US)
$ 24.95 (CAN)
BOOK #: 274812

Design Ideas for Home Storage is loaded with color photographs and lots of consumer-friendly information on providing both everyday and long-term storage for everything. *Paper with flaps.*

Over 350 photographs.
208 pp.
$ 19.95 (US)
$ 24.95 (CAN)
BOOK #: 279491

Design Ideas for Flooring is the ultimate guide to the latest materials, products, and styles in flooring. Over 350 color photographs. *Paper with flaps.*

Over 350 photographs.
208 pp.
$ 19.95 (US)
$ 24.95 (CAN)
BOOK #: 279242

Design Ideas for Home Decorating is a general decorating book that presents design solutions for every room in the house, and for every budget. *Paper with flaps.*

Over 500 photographs.
320 pp.
$ 19.95 (US)
$ 24.95 (CAN)
BOOK #: 279323

Look for these and other fine **Creative Homeowner books** wherever books are sold.
For more information and to order direct, visit our Web site at
www.creativehomeowner.com